ADVANCE PRAISE FOR GETTING HAPPY WITH YOUR BODY

Jill Pagano shares her invaluable wisdom in a way that feels like she is sitting right next to you. Her non-judgmental and compassionate approach empowers you to discover this precious practice of creating a more loving relationship with your body. Jill is clearly in love with the human body and she inspires you to be in love with your body too.

Getting Happy with Your Body pours sweet healing salve into your mind, body, and spirit. It's as if your loving body is talking to you through each page. You'll love how it feels!

~Susan Tate, author of *Wellness Wisdom and Into the Mouths of Babes*, www.susantate.org

Like Jill Pagano herself, Getting Happy with Your Body sparkles with a unique style, deep wisdom, big heart, is easy to get to know and pleasant to be with. Want to live a fully vibrant life? Here's your map.

~Helen Terry, M.Ed., CEO, Soma Ranch, LLC

Finally, the book I've always wanted! The antidote to all the other messages about being at war with your body, Jill Pagano's book is like sitting down with your favorite friend. Her easy and smart application helps you get happy with your body and realize how all these years, your body has carried you, held you, nourished you and loved you, despite how you've talked to her. Make peace. It's worth it!

~Libby Wagner, poet, author and speaker

What a powerful and healing offering this book is! Jill skillfully blends her compelling story, science, structured practices and spirituality to give us a clear road map back into our bodies.

~Deborah Kern, PhD, health scientist, author, speaker

Jill Pagano's gregarious tone, openness about her own body's journey and what it has taught her, and encouraging journal questions create an invitation to a positive, lasting relationship with the body that is sustainable and, far better, joyful.

What Pagano suggests in the title of this book, Getting Happy with Your Body, is so simple, yet it turns a lifetime of cultural and social messaging on its ear. Instead of fighting with our bodies, why not treat it as a partner and ally? This is a must-read for anybody who is ready to live the adage of "happiness comes from within" -- which is so much more magnetic than "no pain, no gain."

~ Melanie McFarland, black belt instructor, Nia Technique®, television critic and writer

Getting Happy with Your Body has so much depth and heart. Jill's personal stories are mixed with compelling argument and deeply powerful life changing tools. Jill offers very clear guidance and creative practices. It left me profoundly grateful to have a gift of offering a space for women and men to let go of thinking and enter into sensing and feeling their body.

~Kelly Atkins, founder of Kai® Integrated Fitness www.KaiMoves.com

Getting Happy with Your Body

How to Live In, Learn From, and Love Your Body Once and For All.

JILL PAGANO

Getting Happy with Your Body: How to Live In, Learn From and Love your Body Once and For All.

This book is meant to support and guide readers and contains education and advice. It is not intended for medical or mental health advice and should be used to supplement rather than replace regular care by your healthcare professionals. All efforts have been made to ensure accuracy of the information contained in this book as of the date of publication. The publisher and the author disclaim liability for any medical or mental health outcomes that may occur as a result of the advice given in this book.

Edited by: Nip and Tuck Editing, Elise Kloter
Cover Photo: Amy Shamblen on Unsplash
Photography By: Native Light Photo
Book Design and Layout: Kieanna McCloud
Library of Congress, Cataloging-in-Publication Data

Pagano, Jill
Getting Happy with Your Body: How to Live In, Learn From and Love Your Body Once and For All./Jill Pagano
p. cm.
ISBN: 978-1-7329946-0-7 (pbk)
ISBN: 978-1-7329946-1-4 (ebk)

1. Health & fitness - Healthy living 2. Self help - Personal growth 3. Body, mind, spirit - Inspirational - Personal growth

Printed in The United States

CONTACT THE AUTHOR
Jill Pagano
The Happy Body Habit®
www. JillPagano.com
Email: jill@JillPagano.com

DEDICATION

Getting Happy with your Body is dedicated to all human beings and to the magical bodies we live in. And specifically to the two in my daily world, who are my greatest inspiration: Delaney and Kellen.

CONTENTS

ACKNOWLEDGMENTS

When the student is ready the teacher appears. I've spent a good portion of my life ready, as I've been blessed with inspiring teachers who have expanded my views, understanding, and possibilities.

With full appreciation and gratitude for my teachers…

Kari Anderson, for mentoring me in taking my love of movement into a professional teaching career. **Peggy Hackney**, for helping me become embodied by making connections in my own body. **Geneen Roth**, whom I have yet to meet, for shedding light on our important relationship with food like no other has. **Mary Susan Corrado**, for introducing me to mind-body connection in the very early days when few had heard of (let alone pronounced correctly) Pilates. **Debbie Rosas and Carlos Rosas**, co-creators of The Nia Technique ®, for over twenty years of education on somatic movement and self-mastery. Thanks also for tilting my world with one simple invitation "to sense." **Sue Hitzmann**, for expanding my world of self-care to include "you can't get out of pain by creating pain"—words I live by. **Gary Ward**, for restoring my faith in educational integrity, my feet, and introducing me to the elegance of Finding Centre. And, **Gil Hedley Ph.D**, for providing a welcoming and unparalleled space for fulfilling my childhood dream of exploring the human body and guiding me on my "somanaut" journey.

With full appreciation and gratitude for the support…

A huge thank you to **Elise Kloter** for "Nipping and Tucking" words, sentences and chapters with what felt like endless edits. Your humor got me through. For my artistic director, **Kieanna McCloud**, thank you for creating beauty with my website, promotional materials, and especially the book design. To **Libby Wagner**, thank you for being the first to tell me "You can." To **Sindy Todo** for always sharing your magic mojo. To **Dot Chase**, for the long haul; you've been there from the early days of leg warmers and cassette tapes. **Susan Tate**, for always showing up with love. And **Jennifer Lucero-Earle**, for sharing your Arcana gifts and fanning my flicker of desire into a flame of boldness.

With love and gratitude for my family…

To my deceased parents, **Bill and Florence**, who died when I was less than ten years old, I live your legacy of love and elegance. To my sister, **Lynn,** for your encouragement, love, and hours of discussion helping me discern what getting happy with your body means. To **Bill and Marilyn** and their children, thank you for making us a family of seven. You made all the difference in my life. To **Mike,** for co-parenting with love and respect. To **Joel**, for keeping the lights on even while I was burning the midnight oil, and for your patience and endless tech support that kept me from throwing the keyboard. But mostly for your daily acts of love. To my daughter **Delaney** and son **Kellen**, for reminding me, through your own pursuits and ambitions, that I can, too. You are my greatest love. Nothing compares to the joy of being your mother.

And to You…

To thirty years of **clients and class students**, thank you for the privilege. Thank you for space at the front of the room to share what I learn and love. This book blooms from your seeds.

To **the readers,** thank you. Thank you for looking at the cover, reading the title and being willing to step towards co-creating happiness with your body. Let us continue this adventure together. And lastly, to **my body,** praise to you. Thank you for being my ultimate teacher.

INTRODUCTION

My Story

When I was nearly seven years old, my mom took me to a matinee called *The Fantastic Voyage*. The story was about a team of people purposely miniaturized and injected into a brilliant scientist's body in order to fix a clot in his brain and save his life. The movie was thrilling to me! The team traveling through various parts of his body was mesmerizing. I can remember thinking, "I wish I could go inside the body."

Of course, as a child I didn't understand the foresight of my wish and how I would dedicate most of my adult life to my own fantastic voyage.

January 9, 2018

I am by myself at a getaway resort near Blaine, Washington, at the northern border of Washington State and Canada. My overnight bag is filled with the necessary rain gear for long beach walks, an array of my favorite pens and mechanical pencils, and, as a long-time journal writer, a few blank journals.

Why am I here? What am I looking to discover? Unlike may people booked at a resort, I'm not specifically looking to relax. After recently selling my exercise/movement studio of five years, The Center for Movement & Healing, it's not relaxation I'm looking for.

What I'm looking for is quiet. My life up to this point has been teeming with activity, to-dos and responsibility. I've come here to listen, to slip into the quiet, so I can once again hear my deep inner voice guide me. It's daunting. I feel like I need a hearing aid.

What will I hear within my room's elegantly-rustic four walls? Will cuddling up on the deck with a wool blanket while staring out at the beautiful bay crack me open enough to hear that faint whisper?

For the last two years I've been anxious. Well, antsy, with an unusual dose of dissatisfaction. Something is off. I haven't been feeling right. I've been teaching the same body of work for nearly 20 years. And yet for the last two years, I feel like I've grown out of it. I feel "done." Something deep inside me is saying "stop." At least for now.

It's terrifying. And that is why I am here gazing through the misty drizzle: to wrestle with this whisper, "Stop teaching."

Apparently there is something else I need to be doing. Truth be told, deep within I have an inkling as to what I am here to do next. I can look back at decades-old journals and read my desire to write a book and "share what I learn and love."

But there was marriage and two amazing babies that joyfully redirected my life, leaving me simultaneously distracted and fulfilled. The last 18 years have been a whirlwind of monotony and magic—a steady flow of memories, one year after another. I've been home for my kids; except now, as teenagers, they aren't home much anymore.

And that is where my life sits now. My daughter's last year of high school. Last homecoming dance. Last high school soccer season. So many "lasts." Her brother just two years away from leaving the nest.

With these endings come new beginnings. Not just for them, but for me, too.

Sitting here in my room, I am not only grieving the inevitable empty nest, I am simultaneously yearning for a clearer sense of what's next. This big consideration has been pressing its face against the window of my soul and repeatedly asking, "What are you here to do? What is your next?"

I stare back blankly.

Nine months later, reading over my initial notes of that weekend, you'd think I was a stay-at-home or work-in-the-home-only mom. That's only part of the picture. The entire picture is I spent my primary parenting years also running my own businesses. There were a few: I worked for health clubs teaching dance fitness and yoga, and then taught additional classes under my own business name. For a period of two years, I enjoyed writing, producing and co-hosting a radio show called *The Sisters of Sizzle Talk Radio*. Being a trainer for a somatic movement program led me to open my own studio, leading six-day educational intensives. Each of these ventures involved inspiring people to embrace learning and loving not only their bodies but also their lives, and sharing my deep belief that moving our bodies is powerful medicine.

My career story starts way back in college when I taught aerobics to my sorority sisters. This was a time period influenced by the pop culture of the late 80's, paved by movies like *Flashdance* and *Fame*, and Jane Fonda's ever-popular exercise videos. *Shape Magazine* was a regular at the grocery store checkout aisle, touting fitness over fashion. By the early 90's, Nike's iconic campaign "Just Do It" was in full swing. Generation X was more fitness-conscious than Baby Boomers, with a definite lean towards vanity. Eating high carbs but no fat was the craze, and everyone I knew was taking aerobic dance classes. I was there during what felt like the biggest wave of fitness revolution this country has ever seen. No yoga or Pilates studios. No CrossFit on every corner or outdoor boot camps in your neighborhood parks. In 1992, exercise was all about dance fitness classes. I'm not talking a studio of ten to twenty people. No, I'm talking, at the height of this era, upwards of fifty men and women in a room jamming to professionally-mixed music (cassette tapes!) led by a perfectly fit instructor through exhaustive dance routines, only to finish with floor work, endless sit ups, push-ups, and leg lifts.

I got my start at one of Seattle's top aerobic studios. I had the privilege of learning from the owner, a well-respected fitness-industry presenter and educator who took the art of teaching of the workday, I was so ready to move. I needed exercise. Specifically, dance exercise.

I needed to lead the almighty sweat. To be in my "target heart rate zone." To feel the burn. To Just Do It. I loved working out and I loved teaching dance aerobics. On some level, dance aerobics reconnected me with my college years dancing for the University of Idaho's dance theater department and dance team. While teaching at the gym, members started asking me to personally train them. They wanted to be fit and look like me, asking me if I could transform their body to look like mine. "How can I get your legs?" Um, from my mother?

For a while I taught aerobics, trained clients, and held on to my nine to five corporate gig. Then I took the leap and left my desk job. I was thrilled! I had a degree in Communication and Public Relations and only a certificate to teach aerobics from a fitness association. So when I began training clients privately, I took myself on a crash course in all things body. For the next six years, I went to every workshop and convention I could afford. I read consumer and trade magazines. I studied with exercise physiologists and earned a certificate in specialized personal training.

My business evolved as I became the go-to trainer for clients' more complex ailments. Not just regulars who wanted to lose a little fat, or get in shape for summer's bikini season. I was now creating post-rehab fitness programs for members who experienced mastectomies, ACL repairs, hip replacements and arthritis. These were members not only wanting to get back in shape, but looking to get back into their body after traumatic injuries or illness. Going the traditional route of lifting weights and running on treadmills was not going to work for this motley crew, who quickly became like family. With the newness of the personal training industry, education for trainers, especially specialized trainers like myself, was limited. So as my client load grew more complex, I did what most entrepreneurs do to fill a void: I did what came naturally to me—I learned by moving my body.

I love the human body and I love to move. I can't remember a time when I didn't love to move. As a toddler I would dance in front of the TV at family gatherings. I was so on the move my family nicknamed me Shaky Jake. During high school, I turned our basement into my own mini-dance and exercise studio with a mini-trampoline, rubber tubing, weights, and a cassette player. Living in rural Idaho, I spent hours dancing in my basement, going on runs with my black lab, Frick, or hitting tennis balls against the side of the barn.

I found my love. I loved to move.

So, when it came time to learn more for my rehabbing-specialty clients, I looked to my college years as a dancer for guidance. I began to study the type of movement training dancers used to keep their bodies strong and healthy. At the time, these forms were unheard of to the general public. But the dance community had engaged with these forms of "alternative exercise" for years, if not decades, before they would become more mainstream. Excited at the possibility of helping my clients even more, I dove deeply into being a student again. I studied Pilates before people knew how to pronounce it. I experimented with Feldenkrais' Awareness through Movement®, which touts mindful movement. I studied with Peggy Hackney, a treasured educator who introduced me to Bartenieff Fundamentals℠ and movement patterning. I dabbled in Gyrotonics®, spiraling my body with the help of intricate machinery.

After each class or course, I would bring my experience back to my clients, back to the crew that motivated me to seek more for them while filling up my own toolbox. It was a privilege I'll always be grateful to have experienced. The trust they placed literally in my hands and body was invaluable. Together, as I grew to understand the human body, they grew to better understand their own bodies.

Before I knew it, training thirty-plus clients a week and teaching six to nine aerobic classes a week was starting to take a toll on me. I was young, under 30 still, and in elite athlete physical shape. In my few off-hours, I enjoyed hiking in Seattle's Olympic mountain range. I'd rock climb and camp on the weekends. I'd water ski at sunrise on Lake Washington during the Seattle summers and cross-country ski and snow camp in the winters. I was living my passion: to move. I loved the outdoors as much as coming inside to be with my clients and teaching my classes.

Then I started to lose energy. At first I thought it was just a lack of sleep, too much burning the candle at both ends. Well, that candle ended up being the Epstein Barr virus my body couldn't fight. Then it was a case of shingles. Those two viruses seemed to open the floodgates to problems, one after the other: thoracic outlet syndrome, shoulder impingement, chronic shin splints and plantar fasciitis. While I was working hard and playing big, my body was struggling to keep up. I'll never forget visiting a doctor and reading her chart notes: "Showing signs of anorexia nervosa with tendencies to compulsively exercise."

What?

I was a fitness professional. My industry was surrounded by teachers battling through injuries. I was a warrior, just like them, wearing my body like a badge of fitness perfection. I passionately taught people how to be fit and healthy. I was a shining example of the virtues of fitness. Right?

I was so busy teaching aerobic dance, learning more, sharing with my clients and playing in the great outdoors, I simply got in the habit of being the boss of my body. I told my body what I needed to get done. I told my body what I wanted to do and what it would have to endure for me.

And my body did all that I asked, until it just couldn't anymore.

Even though it was asking me to slow down for months, maybe years, I wasn't listening. Truth be told, I didn't even know how to listen. My communication with my body was one-direction, with everything coming from me. I never took the time to understand how to be receptive to my body or how to listen to what it needed or desired. Even though I was a professional fitness instructor at the height of my career with a body to show for it, I had no idea how to pay attention to my body and no idea it was breaking down because of what I was putting it through.

I thought all this illness and injury was, well, normal.

I knew I needed to do something different but I had no idea what that would be. So I kept doing what I knew. I went to another well-regarded fitness convention, this one in Las Vegas. In the early mornings before the seminars began, master teachers would offer workouts, which of course, I attended. I was drawn to a Nia class called "Guts and Grace," which was a blend of dance, martial arts and mindfulness.

At 7am the next morning I showed up to the large, bland hotel conference room with that dull, commercial carpet and a big, somewhat-fake-looking chandelier hanging in the center. I'm sure during elegant dinners the room could be dressed up lovely. But today, without any décor, it felt sterile and lifeless; except for the music playing in the background. "What's with that music?" I thought to myself. It wasn't the traditional canned fitness music with synthesized sounds. The music in the ballroom that morning sounded, well, musical. There were lyrics, harmony, rhythm and, oddly enough, real instruments. I made my way into the room to the two co-creators of the class. The male teacher had long shoulder-length brown hair. The female teacher's hair was closely shaved to her head and dyed nearly-see-through white. They both wore colorful exercise leotards and tights and adorned themselves with lots of jewelry. And they both had warm smiles that extended to their eyes.

This whole scene was odd to me. Where was the loud, beat-driven music? What's with all this colorful clothing? And why are they barefoot?

Then they invited us to take off our shoes. And I thought, "Toto, I'm not in Kansas anymore."

Throughout class, the teachers had invited us to sense our bodies. They also encouraged us to dance expressively. When it came time to do floor work, they called it floor play.

Throughout class, they repeatedly encouraged us to find the "joy" in our body.

Joy? Sense my body? Express myself? Play? Move "my own way and in my own time"? I was accustomed to exercising in order to sweat, burn calories, and get stronger. I liked doing that but never considered my movement to be joyful.

To my biggest surprise, this one-hour-long experience flipped a switch deep inside me. It woke the sleeping giant. In that dull convention ballroom with 100 plus other fitness professionals, I felt my body in a new way. I felt my body move a new way, a way I hadn't felt since being a playful child. I can only describe the experience akin to returning home. For fleeting moments in that class, I, Jill, experienced being with my body. And once I felt that connection, I wanted more.

Little did I know the profound impact that one class would have on my career and my life.

This book is an outpouring of the next twenty years: my journey of exploring how to maintain and strengthen the unique connection between myself and my body. And to learn from, live in and love my body, inspiring others to as well.

On January 10, 2018, after spending a quiet night at the resort, I awoke ready to journal. Outside, the cloud cover created a mysteriously still and silver landscape. As often happens when I begin journaling, I received a download. On this silver-toned January day at my home away from home, I received the message, "Jill, you help people get happy with their body."

This book is my first written adventure into sharing my philosophy and processes for getting happy with your body. It's part love story, part guide and part workbook.

Getting Happy with your Body brings together the three necessary ingredients to start your new journey with your body: You, Your Relationship and Your Body.

In Section One you'll discover what it means for you to get happy with your body. You'll explore what's getting in the way of getting happy with your body and look at how your upbringing, family history and life experiences influence how you think and feel about your body.

In Section Two we'll discuss developing a relationship mindset by which to cultivate a meaningful relationship with your body, just like you do with friends and family.

Section Three lays out the Be with your Body Practice: how to listen to your body and make choices that feel good.

As an avid journal keeper, I've incorporated Ask Yourself and Journal segments. There are a few home practices, too. Enjoy the process! Invite in your curiosity and leave behind drawing harsh conclusions. Let yourself be fascinated as your stories flow out of you and into your writing. Bring honesty and compassion to yourself and your body. Do your best to release any shame; instead appreciate how you got here while feeling excited for what's to come.

Feel free to pick pieces of the book that work for you and dive deeply into them. Leave parts of the book behind if they don't resonate with you right now. And above all, do what you can to soothe your inner critic, and instead choose to celebrate your desire to learn from, live in, and love your body!

SECTION I

Getting to Know Your Happy

"Cry. Forgive. Learn. Move on. Let your tears water the seeds of your future happiness."

— Steve Maraboli

CHAPTER 01

What Is Getting Happy With Your Body?

Imagine feeling good about your body. Imagine having a sense of how to address your body's changing needs. Imagine being able to decipher your body's subtle aches and pains and turn them into greater understanding and solutions. Imagine a time in the near future when you feel comfortable in, confident with, and relaxed about your body. A time when you are willing and able to listen to your body and make choices that feel good to your body and satisfying to you. And perhaps most importantly, a time when criticizing your body is a thing of the distant past.

Sound like a dream? In a way, it is. It is my dream for you. But it is not a dream that is lofty or unattainable. This dream is within your reach. If you are curious, excited, and willing, you can learn how to transform your dream into a day-to-day reality.

But this dream is going to take some conscious attention. You may even call it work. I like to call it practice. It's also going to take a willingness to shift your consciousness to accept that if you want to get happy with your body, you're going to have to build it.

Build what?

You're going to have to build a relationship with your body, just like you develop healthy and loving relationships with others in your life.

That's right—you, with the help of this book, are going to resurrect your relationship with your body. You are going to resurrect the way you understand your body, consider it, and treat it. Once you enter into this type of resurrected relationship with your body, all the struggle, disconnect and discontent will become a faded memory.

Getting happy with your body is an active and ongoing process where you continually consider how your body looks, feels, and performs. And because you are engaging in a relationship with your body, it's a two-sided consideration: How happy are you with your body? And, how happy is your body with you?

Getting happy with your body is ultimately recognizing the relationship you co-create with your body, while doing your very best to honor, learn, and enjoy the entire process of living in a body.

Well, that is ideal.

Respecting the Ebb and Flow

Just like the other relationships you have in your life, getting happy with your body will involve a little give and take. There will be times when you will not feel perfectly connected to, engaged with, or approving of your body. There will be days where your happiness fluctuates. And some days you'll have to actively cultivate a little more happiness juju than other days.

Each day with the privilege of waking up, you have the choice to turn towards and include your body. On most days, with practice, you will. Some days you won't. Some days you may just let your practice slide. During these times, getting happy with your body is more about accepting yourself and your body even when you are feeling low, slow and turned off. You see, creating a practice to cultivating a relationship with your body does accumulate, but it is not strictly accumulative, each and every day. You aren't expected to be on a single trajectory where each day you accumulate more, like rungs on a ladder where each step takes you further up, never slipping backwards. Some days, you'll be super tuned in, while other days you'll find yourself annoyed and disappointed all over again.

Here's my plea: don't let that stop you.

I see this so often. Individuals have a tendency to simply drop the proverbial ball (getting happy with their body) and refuse to pick it up again, until their body is so out of whack, getting back in the game is a last resort. It's like one day forgetting to buy cat food and instead of picking up a bag next time you're at the store, you simply forget you have a cat. You've got an illness, an injury, or twenty extra pounds, and instead of turning towards your body, you simply shut down, turn off and suffer through life. Has anyone seen Kitty—I mean—your body?

What to do? Wake up, pull the sheets off, rise from bed, and start again with "Hello Body." Again and again. No matter how futile that may feel or pathetic that may sound, do it anyway; acknowledge your body at least once each and every day. You say good morning to the important people in your life, so why not start with your body?

Take a deep breath on this one, my friend.

The work you do between you and your body is continual. Getting happy with your body is a fascinating lifelong story you develop between you and your body, a story with no end, just different chapters. You see, even if you are dissatisfied and disappointed with your body, you are still in a relationship with it. Even if that relationship feels more like a battle, or one you'd rather ignore, or feel you don't have time for. Nonetheless, you and your body are in this crazy life together. Whether you cultivate an enjoyable relationship with your body or not, there will come a time when you must help your body, consider its needs, and respond to it. You cannot leave your body behind, at least not while alive. Eventually your body will need your care. It will at some point demand your attention.

How about you not wait until things get Ugly—I think you have a sense of what I mean by capital U Ugly. I'm not describing looks. I'm describing situations. Getting Ugly with your body is taking a fistful of prescription medications whose side effects are as equally damaging as the illness you are trying to heal. Ugly is not being able to move the way you want and enjoy life with friends and family. Ugly is having to make amends and consolations because your body and energy are not up for living fully anymore. Life gets very small and limited when your body is no longer able to take you out into the world, your neighborhood, your backyard, freely and joyfully. All this can happen because a year ago, five years ago, a decade ago, you allowed yourself to stop caring about your body. Or you *didn't decide* to start caring about your body.

Why is this? Why can't you just be happy with your body and call it good—check off the box, cross it off your list, grab the trophy, and move on with your life?

Because you are a living, breathing, evolving, transforming human being. You are in a constant state of ebb and flow.

Crossing something off your list is for objects like milk and bread. You acquire it and move on, put it in the grocery cart and on to the next aisle. Check-mark boxes and lists are not for the day-to-day, scrappy job of living in a relationship with your body. You are perpetually transforming. You conjure, adapt and are constantly recreating. You are who you are, and yet you are recreating yourself all the time with each new stage and chapter of your life. You aren't stagnant and neither is your body.

Your body is in a constant cycle of change, adaption and creation, as are you. Your body truly is different on a cellular level every day, sluffing off and renewing right under your nose. And this renewing continues over days, months, years, decades, until your life ends. There are two evolving elements: your body and you. Which is why, my beloved (and your beloved body), getting happy with your body is a constant recalibration, a constant relationship in flux. It's an evolving dance of give and take between the time you have, the energy you give, and the attention you place on your body and on the relationship with your body. And the great news is your body is everything you could desire in a lifelong partner: responsive, communicative, informative, and solely dedicated to you.

Did you catch that last part—the "solely dedicated to you" part? That is correct; your body is solely dedicated to helping you fulfill your desires, chase your dreams, and live your life.

Even though getting happy with your body may sound like a daunting task, as you create a responsive relationship with your body, you'll reap the benefits of thriving in it. Your state of being will be connected to your body and you'll notice when your relationship needs a little more attention. You'll be able to sense when you've strayed from your body and be ready to return home.

Asking: How Do You Feel Now?

I think it is a rare occurrence when we step back, sit down, and truly consider what getting happy with our body looks and feels like to us and our body. We are so accustomed to thinking five pounds, a half-marathon, or a size smaller will finally give us the satisfaction we want. And any of those may, rightfully so, make us feel great. But what about the next day, the next month, or the next year? Are you always chasing another achievement in order to feel satisfied with your body? If so, this can be dangerous territory because at some point, at some age, your body may not be able to do what you want or need it to do in order to feel good about it. Attaching your personal happiness to specific outcomes can lead to unnecessary disappointment and dissatisfaction when instead you can learn to live and respond to your needs while respecting your body's abilities today.

This happened to me a few years ago when an unexpected hip injury sidelined me from dancing, my favorite form of exercise that also feeds my soul. Actually, the hip injury kept me from any exercise, even easy walking. Within a few months the injury led to aggravating a preexisting bulging disc in my lower back. Oh my, before I knew it two years went by without consistent exercise. Not being able to do what I enjoyed with my body really forced me to rethink how I was with my body. I remember years ago sharing with a client, "Sure, I'm happy with my body. I'm lucky, it has always done what I wanted." Well, that all changed over those two years and I had to rediscover a way to be happy with myself and my body, even when I was frustrated with how my body was performing. Being in this situation enabled me to take a deeper look at my own expectations and find a new way to love myself and my body, even though I didn't like the situation I was in with it.

As you embark on the path to rekindling the relationship between you and your body, you'll want to have a sense of where you currently are with your body and what you desire moving forward. Not so you can judge yourself for your shortcomings or disappointments. Quite the contrary. Instead, so you can recognize your progress and transformation. Recognizing your current state of being will help you create a marker to reflect on, especially times when your progress feels stagnant.

Most clients share with me that they are frustrated by how they look, confused by how their bodies act, and disappointed by how their bodies feel. Or maybe they are disappointed by how they look, annoyed with how their bodies act, or disheartened by how their bodies feel. The adjectives may change, but the sentiment is always the same: I don't like how my body looks, acts or feels.

Whether you are frustrated by an extra 10 (or 50) pounds, an illness or injury, or something completely unavoidable like aging or going through menopause, it's quite possible and highly probable that you have "big" feelings about how your body IS right now.

Go ahead. How do you feel, right now?

I'm______________________________ about how my body looks.

I'm ______________________________ about how my body acts or performs.

I'm ______________________________ about how my body feels.

How would you like to feel in the future?

I'd like to feel ______________________________ about how my body looks.

I'd like to feel ______________________________ about how my body acts or performs.

I'd like to feel ______________________________ about how my body feels.

Ask Yourself and Journal...

What is getting in the way of you being happy with your body—today?

How long have you been feeling this way? You weren't always unhappy with your body, were you?

Getting Happy with your Body Is:

1) Dependent on discovering and describing what your happy is.

2) Never stagnant: The practice is as alive and adaptable as you and your body.

3) Relational: Depends on both you AND your body.

Defining: What is your Happy?

Happy, to me, is uniquely-sensed contentment. More effervescent than simply satisfied. Sunny with a dash of lightheartedness and fascination. When I consider the act of getting happy with my body, I sense myself and my body spiraling up with contentment and optimism. Yes, happiness is an emotion, but in this program, it is not only an emotion for me to have. I sense my body feels happy, too. And I can be happy with the relationship between me and my body.

Happy Body Assessment

If you are ready to get happy with your body, we're going to jump right in and start with the Happy Body Assessment (HBA). The HBA is all about you checking in and taking note as to what is going on in the context of your life right now. What's your happy? Where are you investing your time and energy? What are you placing your attention on and are you creating situations that can support your happiness?

Start by asking yourself, "What's my happy"? Not your doctor's happy. Not your spouse's. Not your rack of clothes, two sizes too small. Right now, today, I ask you to consider what does getting happy with your body mean to you?

Ask Yourself and Journal...

What do you **feel** like (physically) when you have a happy body? You can start this inquiry with, "I physically feel_____." For example: *I physically feel comfort and ease in my body. I am able to move freely. I physically feel comfort in my feet. I am energetic even after a long day of work.*

How does your body perform or **act** when you have a happy body? "My body is able to ____." For example: *My body is able to bring groceries up the stairs easily. My body is able to eliminate waste without taking laxatives. My body is able to run with more comfort.*

What does your body **look** like when you have a happy body? "My body looks ____." For example: *My body looks healthy and right-sized for my frame. My body looks athletic. My posture looks youthful.*

Now explore these questions using a creative technique called Mind Mapping. Mind Mapping is a free-flowing way to use simple words and phrases to explore a particular subject. Our subject is **"My Happy Body."** Put that in the center. Ask yourself how you want your body to feel, look and act/perform.

Here's my mind map…

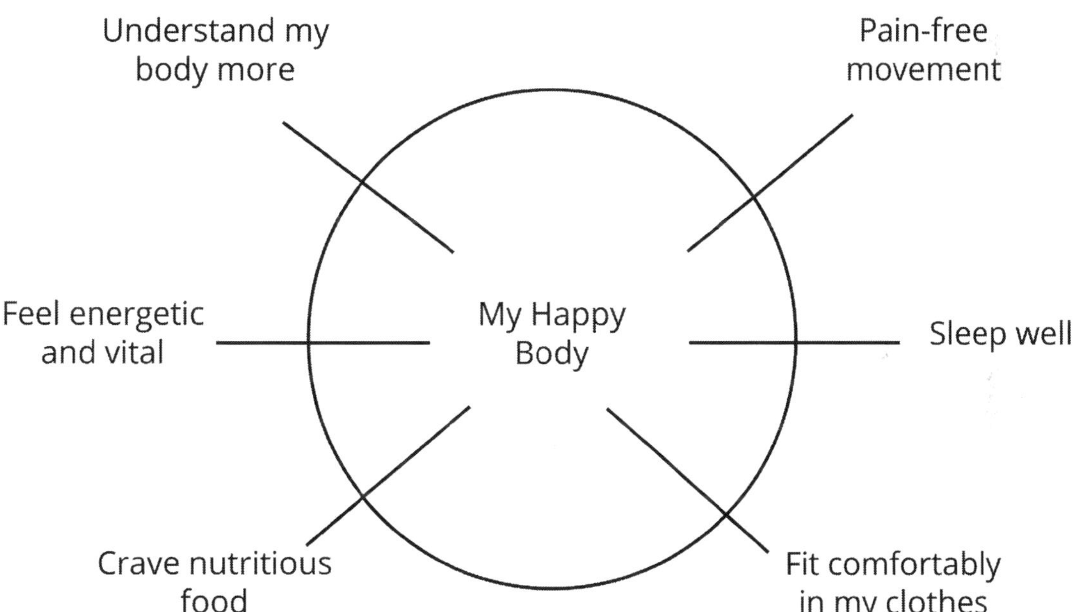

Create Your Happy Body Mind Map

(here or use another piece of paper)

In order to begin your journey towards getting happy with your body, take four words or phrases from your mind map that resonate with you the most. These words are important desires you want to embody as you get happy with your body.

For me, getting happy with my body means:

1) Being able to move, pain-free

2) Fitting comfortably in my clothes

3) Having a better understanding of what's going on in my body

4) Having the energy I need for the life I desire

Now list yours:

1)

2)

3)

4)

Let's assess where you are today. Take your four words and put them on the happiness scale. The unhappy emoji means not at all present in your life, and the happy emoji means 100% present. Mark where you are today.

The Happy Body Assessment Scale

Here's my Happy Body Scale…

1. *Pain-free movement*

2. *Comfortable in my clothing*

3. *Understanding my body*

4. *Energy for my life*

The Happy Body Assessment Scale

Now it's your turn. Fill in the blank with your four words or phrases. Mark an "**X**" where you feel you are on the scale.

1. ____________________

2. ____________________

3. ____________________

4. ____________________

My Story

Based on the Happy Body Assessment, we can create an assessment, or story, of where we are and where we want to go to get happy with our body. Here's my story:

My markers for getting happy with my body are to have a body that moves more with less pain, where my clothes fit comfortably. I want a body that I understand and that provides me with the energy for the life I desire. You'll see from my charting, I am currently satisfied with my body's ability to move pain-free, about a 7 on my scale. For the last few months I've been enjoying a new-to-me workout after a nearly 24-month hiatus from exercise. Enjoyable, regular exercise has helped my clothes fit more comfortably (also a 7 on my scale). Striving to continually heal from a previously injured hip and low back, I'm still learning which exercises keep them feeling good (a 5 on my scale). I've recently noticed I'm feeling less energetic than I desire (about a 4 on my scale), which is why I've been seeing a naturopath and have started a new supplement protocol.

Using your scale as a guide, write your story here or use another sheet of paper.

Taking Another Approach

For some of you, considering what getting happy with your body means to you may feel too distant and unattainable. It may be difficult for you to excavate what getting happy with your body looks or feels like for you. If that is your case, there is another way to approach this exercise: flip the coin and do the opposite. If one side of the coin is what you are moving towards in order to get happy with your body, the flip side of the coin is what keeps you from being happy with your body. Generally, I like you to focus on what you desire. However, if getting clear on what you DON'T desire helps you get clear on what you DO, then I'm all for taking a different approach. Repeat the exercise from above. This time ask yourself how you don't want your body to feel, act/perform and look like. Create your Mind Map, your four markers, and assess where you rank today with what you don't want to feel.

For example my list would be I don't want to:

1) *Move with pain*

2) *Feel uncomfortable in my tight clothing*

3) *Be confused about my body*

4) *Feel low-energy*

Managing Your Time, Attention, Energy, and Interest

In any relationship you have offerings—what you give to another. Time, attention, and energy are all gifts you bring to invest in a healthy relationship. The quantity and quality of these three gifts determines the nature of the relationship. A greater investment of time, energy, and attention will equate to a more involved relationship. The quality of your time, energy and attention will determine the quality of the relationship. If I invest all my time, all my energy, and all my attention into my body, I can become obsessed. If the attention I give my body is filled with negative thoughts, my relationship will not be a supportive one. So not only the amount but also the quality of our time, energy, and attention are three important ingredients. You get to decide what is just right for you and your body. Let's look at these individual "ingredients" more closely.

Your Time

How much time do you give and gift your body? Do you take time to make yummy food? Do you eat slowly enough to enjoy your food? Do you take time for walks in nature or other activities that bring you joy? Do you take time to visit your doctor for annual checkups?

Or is time your enemy? Do you often catch yourself saying, "I don't have time"?

Here's the thing—we all have time, until we don't. We don't know when our time runs out. What matters is what you are doing with the time you have. Now, there are certainly periods in our life where we are heavy with responsibility and time for ourselves is at a minimum. When this is the case we can invest more in Attention and Energy. So even if your time is short, you can still pay attention to your body with a quick check-in, for example, when you are stuck in traffic. Sitting on that freeway is a perfect opportunity to place your attention, for a brief moment, on a deep breath. Or relax your grip on the steering wheel. Do a little spinal twist while at a stoplight. You have time throughout your day to invest in your body. Don't worry if you don't have two hours every morning for a perfect sit-down breakfast and a fitness class. Short moments, taken consistently over a lifetime, add up to big benefits.

Ask Yourself and Journal...

How much time do you invest in your body?

Is that time in larger chunks, like working out for an hour, only to ignore your body the rest of the day? Or does a 10-minute walk help set you up to be connected to your body throughout the morning?

How much time do you invest in your body, even when you are in the midst of other responsibilities (for example, doing a few stretches at your desk or taking a short walk during your lunch break)?

Your Attention

Energy follows Attention...where you place your attention, your greatest amount of energy will follow.

What do you place your attention on throughout the day? Now, that is a BIG question because we are usually flipping from one responsibility to another: first at work, typing on the keyboard, and the next moment answering a phone. We move our attention around, like a flashlight looking for something in the dark. Unfortunately, we forget to place our attention, our flashlight, on ourselves and our body. Because we get caught up in giving our attention away to outside responsibilities (other people, our work, our kids), we miss out on when our body is calling for our attention. Ever sit in a position at a long meeting only to finally notice your back is really hurting? Or what about being so deep in concentration that you don't notice your body really needs to go to the bathroom—like now!

Attention is where we can make huge strides in developing a relationship with our body. And attention doesn't have to take a lot of time. I find healthy awareness and loving attention is the one area my clients can make the biggest difference in cultivating a better relationship with their body at a very low cost. Attention doesn't cost a lot of time or money. Attention is a discipline of the mind and you can craft your awareness with more consciousness and intention.

Ask Yourself and Journal...

Throughout your day, how much attention do you put on your body?

Consider what type of attention you bring to your body. Is it punitive, loving, or filled with discontent?

When I look at social media for an hour each day, I am choosing to give and place my attention on something. My son coming in and asking for help with his homework is asking for my attention. What responsibilities are currently demanding your attention? Are they demanding your attention or are you giving your attention away?

Your Energy

Let's check in with your energy. Years ago the word "energy" may have come across as a little out of the mainstream. However, I find people are more in tune with energy than they realize. "She has a lot of energy" (amount of energy), or "his energy is really positive" (type of energy). We can tell when someone raises our energy because we feel good around them. And likewise, we usually want to spend less time around someone with unpleasant energy. We have the ability to notice amounts of energy as well as types of energy.

Now, let's consider your amount of energy. How much energy do you bring to the relationship between you and your body? Is your body an afterthought, a leftover consideration, after you've burned your energy elsewhere? Or are you willing to invest more energy into learning about your body and how to feel better living in it?

Consider also the type of energy you bring to your body, ranging from positive attributes to negative. What quality of energy are you bringing to your body? Is it playful or inquisitive? Or is the energy you bring usually critical of your body?

How much energy am I bringing to my body (quantity)?

What type of energy am I bringing to my body (quality)?

Your Interest

How interested are you in your body and in cultivating a relationship with your body? Some of us have a natural interest in the human body, like a hobby, while others don't. I believe it is equally important to recognize what your natural interest and enthusiasm levels are in regards to taking care of your body.

If your interest level is low, how could you approach your body to become more interested? For example, if science is fascinating to you, how could you use science to cultivate more interest towards your body? Approaching your body through a scientific lens may spark your interest. If you are a deeply spiritual person, could you weave a sense of your body into your spiritual practice? Perhaps you find praying to be a valuable part of your life. Could walking be a form of connecting to the divine?

All too often, I find people limit the ways they connect to their body. They think it has to be through the traditional channels of diet and exercise. Like the "I need more exercise, so I'll join a gym" mentality, even though they dislike the stale environment of a fitness center. Instead, they may be more interested in playing outside, exploring and enjoying nature. I suggest, as you continue getting happy with your body, you consider not only how interested you are, but also how you can raise your interest by marrying your body with other activities and lifestyle choices you currently enjoy.

Ask Yourself and Journal...

How would you describe your current interest level in your body?

Are you interested due to a single objective? (losing weight, decreasing pain, lowering your blood pressure)?

What other interests do you have that could also involve your body?

Realizing It's about You…but Not Only You

Your ability to adjust and work with time, attention, energy and interest are greatly influenced by two factors: the people in your life and the responsibilities you bear. There are people you love (and don't) and responsibilities you accept (and those you wish you hadn't) that greatly affect your available time, energy and attention. Some of this is to be expected. After all, most of you are not solitary monks living on a hilltop in isolation, seeking enlightenment. You have work, friends, social circles, and volunteer organizations.

If your response to the topic of time, attention and energy is simply, "ha, I don't have any," or "my life is not my own," then use this as your wakeup call. Getting happy with your body (and your life) may elude you until you take responsibility for how, and with whom, you choose to invest and spend your time, energy and attention. Take this opportunity now to look at your current responsibilities and people in your life and ask yourself, "Is my relationship with this person contributing to my life?" "Are the responsibilities I'm agreeing to of value to me?"

Here's something I hope is reassuring to you. The smallest shift in people and responsibilities can shake up your time, attention and energy in big ways. I'm not saying you have to wipe the slate clean and cut off ties from everything and everyone in your life in order to get happy with your body. Consider how to better serve your body by mindfully crafting what you do and who you do it with. I invite you to observe yourself and your day-to-day activities. Start by making small shifts in what you say "yes" and "no" to. Get clearer about who you are hanging out with and their effect on you. Then return to consider how your time, attention and energy can be better invested.

Ask Yourself and Journal...

Are you allowing certain people, even those you love, to get in the way of getting happy with your body?

What responsibilities are getting in the way of you investing time, attention or energy to getting happy with your body?

What could be a small shift in your responsibilities that could allow you to invest more in getting happy with your body?

CHAPTER 02

What Is Getting In Your Way?

We want to be happy with our bodies. We want to stop obsessing over the last five pounds. We want to eat without scrutinizing every morsel of food for calories or fat content. We'd like to feel comfortable in our skin and right-sized for our physical frame and comfort. And for many, we want to finally put an end to the ongoing ugly, negative, or catty commentary in our minds, so we can finally feel satisfied with our bodies.

I know you have been *trying.* Goodness knows no matter what race, gender, sexual orientation or religious beliefs—*you've been trying.* No matter where you live, how much money you make, or who you hang out with—you have been trying to get right with your body. And it isn't just you, is it? Certainly you have a friend, sister, spouse or co-worker that has also been trying.

You've invested time (oh boy, yes), money (your hard-earned cash and credit), and energy (giving it your all!) looking for the magic formula to finally be happy with your body.

And you've made progress. And then lost that progress. You've gained some great information and have swiftly become confused by more great information. You've had feelings of incredible success and suffered from feeling like a failure. I hear all the time, "I know what I *should* do, if only I *would* do it."

Why do so many of us have this dissatisfaction? How did we get here? We weren't *always* unhappy with our bodies. Were we? Think back—for some of you, way back. Was there ever a time when you felt fine with your body? In fact, maybe you didn't even think about your body AT ALL. It's stunning to consider that once upon a time your body and what you thought about it was completely irrelevant to your happiness, a non-issue.

Do you remember the first poignant instance something happened or someone suggested your body might be less than wonderful? Perhaps you saw a picture or read a magazine article that implied your body could use, well, some improving? Or a specific moment when all of a sudden you began looking at your body differently, perhaps more negatively? Yet, when you landed here on earth, weren't you comfortable in your body for many years? And then something—or many somethings—happened.

Is it you or Everything Else? It's both. Yup, this struggle is about you and what goes on inside of you, mostly between the ears. But it's not only about you. It is about the influences outside of you, the world you live in, which is basically everything else.

The Influence of the Diet and Fitness Industry

Everything Else is the world we live in: society's influence and pressure on us, the time, space and place we show up in each day. The big picture is a bit different for each of us, depending on how we were raised, where we grew up, and the heritage of our upbringing. Cultural norms also change throughout generations. What was a cultural norm for our parents and grandparents is not our experience today. Did our grandparents worry about eating enough superfoods or strengthening their abs? Not likely. Our world is continually shifting and influencing each of us in different ways. But there has been consistent pressure that influences us on a daily basis and fuels our insecurities—the diet and fitness industry.

Our country's multi-billion-dollar, advertisement-laden diet and fitness industry relentlessly promises and promotes quick, easy, inexpensive and painless "fixes" for every dissatisfaction we have with our bodies. Take this pill, join this club, get this surgery, and start this diet—and we will all finally be happy, bubbly, super fit, radiant, and surrounded by people who love us (with perfect skin, no less!). We've all witnessed the onslaught of commercials comparing the seemingly unattractive, flabby "before" body against the highly-toned, desirable "after" body. The advertisements continue to tout how this particular plan *"saved them from themselves and launched their new-found life...and it was so easy, all you need to do is..."*

Certainly, many programs work, especially when we commit to them. That is until life throws us a little change, like attending a special occasion, celebrating a string of holidays, or being burdened with a stressful life event. Sometimes (uh, a lot of times), we justify our diversion from the program as simply getting off track. The truth is, most fitness programs and diet plans don't teach us how to be flexible; how to adapt when life's bumps get in the way or burdens becomes too much to bear. So we gain the weight back, lose our motivation, shame and blame our lack of fortitude, and swear that next time, next program, next workout—when life doesn't intervene—we'll do better. These programs and plans fail us due to their very nature of being either ON or OFF. Succeeding or failing.

I see this profusely every January. Zombie-eyed from a holiday-season sugar rush, the mainstream mass eagerly awaits the holy holiday—January 1st (or maybe the 3rd—after all, we do need to start on a Monday). On this holy day, Americans return to the diet and fitness industry's magic formula: eat right and exercise. Thank goodness they got the gift of workout gear, the latest kitchen gadget, and a gym membership. Because this year, it is going to be different. Not only will they find the just-right plan, but they will also be the kind of person who STICKS with it. This year. Yup, this is THE year.

Yes, like clockwork, another January (or June) comes and a new season of hopefuls begin again, all full of promise, ready to invest their time, hard-earned money, and energy into another program they hope will bring the results they crave. And that is when they begin looking for their Prince Charming.

Waiting for Prince Charming

Hoping for a magic plan, program or pill is like desperately awaiting our Prince Charming, hanging our forever perfect dream on a fairy tale.

I first learned of the Cinderella Complex when reading Barbara Stanny's book, *Prince Charming Isn't Coming*, which reveals how women wait to be financially rescued by their Prince

Charming. That book got me thinking. Do we act similarly with our health and well-being?

How often are we looking for another plan, program or product to finally save us from our dilemma and lead to happily-ever-after with our bodies?

If you are reading this book, you have likely been influenced by the relentless promises of the diet and fitness industry's fairy tale.

You are not alone.

In 2017, the United States fitness industry had nearly 26 billion dollars in annual revenue, as reported by the International Health, Racquet & Sportsclub Association (IHRSA), the world's leading health and fitness association. The US weight loss market ballooned to a record high of close to 66 billion dollars in sales as recorded by Market Data, according to the 38-year-old research company's biannual study on the weight loss market. These astronomical amounts of money are for the United States alone. For one year. These numbers nearly add up to what the United States government spends on Medicare and Health (66 billion) and Transportation (26 billion) combined. Amazing, huh? And still, 70% of Americans are overweight with up to 35% obesity in some states.

All this money, all these revolutionary approaches, and still we are not getting our "happy ending."

Do you feel like the next program, plan or diet will be "the one"? Perhaps even this book?

What's your fairy tale around your body? Write down your happy ending.

List the diet or exercise programs you've participated in. Go online and read the language they use to promote their program. Which benefits attracted you the most? What are or what were you wishing to accomplish?

Navigating Confusing Information

Heaven knows if you've lived longer than two decades, you've experienced the onslaught of confusing information on how to become healthier. Is it time to be a vegan or is it time to do the latest high-protein diet? Is it safe and beneficial to do a week-long cleanse? Is long, slow cardio activity or short bursts of interval training better for fat burning? Each one of us sees a slew of newsworthy health articles spouting the success and promise of certain programs. With this abundance of information, no doubt we throw up our hands in exasperation and huff off into the Land of Overwhelm. When confused between too many choices and not enough reliable information, many brains simply hit TILT and do nothing. "If the professionals can't decide what I should do, then I'll do nothing and avoid choosing." By the way, not choosing is a choice, too.

I've been in the fitness and wellness industry for over 25 years. Yes, I've been part of that billion-dollar behemoth. I've lived long enough to come full circle with many fads and trends. I've witnessed a frenzy over protein diets one year, changing to the popularity of the high complex carbohydrates diet, and back to protein plans, again and again. One minute blueberries are the superfood to eat. Then broccoli. And now acai berries and coconut oil are all the rage. A different year, a different fad, a different expectation! Who even knows what is "best" to eat? And that's not even addressing vitamins, supplements, alternative forms of medicine, or exercise! Yes, these nutritious foods, supplements and exercise have value. Blueberries are as healthy now as they were five years ago.

It is time for a new approach where we focus on our long-term wellbeing by learning to understand our bodies' needs and desires.

Looking Outside Yourself

Herein lies part of the dilemma: We are heavily influenced by advertising and media to look outside ourselves for a solution (the right exercise, the right diet) when I believe solving our body issues is an inside job. We cannot become clear about how to get happy with our bodies by blindly putting our lives in another's hands—whether it be a person, a program or a product.

Have you been looking for a quick-fix solution all along?

Have you been looking for something outside yourself, to bend you into submission?

Or worse yet, looking for someone to "whip you into shape"?

All too often, we place our trust mindlessly in the hands of others, even professionals, to tell us exactly what to do. And sure, we get results. Many of us also get injured. And spend lots of money. And end up disappointed that we weren't able to sustain results. The worst part is, we shame ourselves for being weak and blame ourselves for not having enough willpower, as if willpower was some magical force that cured everything. We finish our sentences with the dreaded phrase of defeat "If only I could... (stop eating this, start eating that, do this...)." Or, "If only I had...(enough time, money, willpower)."

BLAH. Stop the madness!

If I had a magic wand, I would put a moratorium on obsessing over the latest plan or fad that is finally going to fix you and your broken body, or fix you and your fat body, or fix you and your whatever body.

There is no fix. There is you and your body. The fix is not your personal trainer. It is not a weight-loss plan. It is you and your body. I know, that sounds foreign right now. Hang with me and I'll explain.

The more you place power in the hands of another, the less likely you'll sustain your new changes once the other influence is no longer around.

At the start of my personal training career my client Carol came to me looking to lose at least 30 pounds. I saw her twice a week and each time she worked out diligently. As her trainer, I would listen to her talk about her problems with her relationships, her job, and other stresses in her life. Clearly, she was burdened by more than being over her ideal weight. But Carol came in religiously to meet with me each week and even came in on her own to walk on the treadmill and lift weights. After a few months, Carol made absolutely no progress in losing weight. She was stronger on the treadmill and the weight machines but the numbers on the scale hadn't budged. During one of her sessions Carol flippantly said, "Well, I'd probably lose weight if I didn't go home and eat half a cake, like last night."

I didn't know what to say or how to address this issue of eating for reasons other than physical hunger. I talked to a nutritionist on staff and she referred me to Geneen Roth's book, *When Food is Love.* Reading Geneen's exquisite and ground-breaking book opened my eyes to a whole new world of why individuals overeat and sabotage their success. This began my career-long pursuit to understand how being happy with our bodies was less about *what to do* (like diets and exercise) and more about addressing *what keeps us* from being happy with our bodies.

Getting happy with your body is a 100% inside job designed to help you develop a long-term, loving relationship with your body

A relationship.

Not a product.

Not a program.

Not a 30-day plan.

Not a week-long cleanse.

Not eating the latest superfood and expecting super results.

You can decide to date around—even have a one-night stand. But when it comes to your health, you and your body are in it for the long haul. Through sickness and in health, til death do you part. That is a relationship worth acknowledging.

The work of getting happy with your body is ultimately an inside job; meaning you turn inward for more answers and ask even more questions. You begin to work *with* yourself versus *against* your body. You learn about yourself and discover your motivation for true transformation.

So let's do that.

Let me guide you to look to yourself and ask, "How might I be contributing to the unhappiness I have about my body?"

CHAPTER 03

Are You Getting In Your Way?

Looking outside ourselves keeps us from getting happy with our bodies. And as irritated as I am with the sales pitches and promises of the diet and fitness industry, I also recognize we can't blame them for all our health issues or our emotional dis-ease surrounding our bodies.

Becoming satisfied with your body and life is ultimately up to You.

When I write of You, I'm referencing what's going on inside of you. Specifically, your self-talk, beliefs, and personal history, which all influence how You feel and relate to your body, as well as the choices You have and decisions You make. I capitalize You on purpose because I'm referring to You, the grown up You, the one in charge, presiding over and taking responsibility for all of what makes up You: your physical body, your thinking mind, your feeling emotions and your unique spirit.

When you are unhappy with your body, it's possible your overactive mind and fearful emotions gang up on and demote You to you, meaning You are no longer in charge—they are. Imagine this: your mind, emotions, and body are all players in the orchestra of your existence. You are the conductor, leading these individual instruments into creating harmonious music. Sometimes the players of instruments get out of practice, or play sloppily. Sometimes they play too loudly or the wrong notes. They make screeching sounds that interrupt the harmony of the orchestra. Many times, the most undisciplined players ruin the entire piece of music. And so it can go with your mind and emotions. Your mind and emotions (what you think and how you feel about yourself) can ruin your life performance unless You take charge and orchestrate your life. You are in charge of your mind, body, and emotions, and can work toward unifying them to serve your best and highest good.

The most pronounced "internal" roadblocks I see in clients are:

- Harboring a negative mindset about their body
- Genuinely not understanding their body's changing needs
- Struggling with having enough time, energy and money
- A history of memories filled with traumas, embarrassments, and heartbreak, leaving a host of ill-serving stories, beliefs, and conclusions

Believing your Stinkin'-Thinkin'

Stanford University psychologist Carol Dweck popularized the idea of having a mindset. *"A **mindset** is a belief that orients the way we handle situations—the way we sort out what is going on and what we should do."* —Psychology Today; May, 2016.

Your mindset—what your mind is set on—influences how you feel, think and act towards your body. Ironically, something that doesn't seem connected to your physical body can really influence how you think, feel and treat your body.

How can the issues with your body start from seeds in your mind? Consider your desktop computer. You have hardware; for example, the pieces you can physically touch, like the keyboard and the monitor. Then there is the software, the thinking part of your desktop system that runs programs like MS Word or Apple Pages. You can't really touch MS Word, and MS Word needs your desktop computer to be seen, to run. Your keyboard can make some nice tapping sounds but it needs a software system to do its job, too. In this way, hardware and software work quite nicely together. Thinking simplistically, this is how your physical body and your mind interact. Like hardware, your physical body is greatly impacted by your software, your thinking. And so the story goes between your mind and your body.

Your mind and body are separate, yet connected, systems. Your mind, and what you think in your mind, highly influence how you feel and what actions you take with your body.

I propose a misaligned mindset, or stinkin'-thinkin', holds more influence than you may realize. Ever notice how the smallest thing can happen, and all of a sudden, your mind has blown the occurrence into a really big deal? Like okay, you ate a few too many potato chips at the party—and now your mind is berating your lousy self-control and you should not have been trusted to go to that party anyway. Which only leaves you more upset and diving back into food again. After all, you've already "blown it."

Your mind can take harsh judgements and assumptions and twist them into seemingly normal and rational thoughts.

Ever have an unusually negative thought that left you thinking, "Where did that thought come from"? Your mind is a super-absorbent sponge designed to soak up and sort out your environment, experiences, situations, joys and fears. All those impressions load into an alchemical mix of how you think about yourself, the world and others. Your mind can be a tricky place when providing honest observations about your body, one of the internal challenges you may face when getting happy with your body.

Ask Yourself and Journal...

What do you frequently say to yourself about your body?

Is what you tell yourself about your body accurate?

Does your mind keep bringing up the same thought over and over again, like a broken record?

Ignoring your Changing Body

Another challenge to getting happy with your body is that your body is ever-changing! Hey, I get it. A changing body makes it more difficult to know what, in fact, helps your body be happy. For me, one month my body is fine with some light running, and a month later I have a few sore and achy spots that make running feel like a chore. For most of my life I've been able to eat whatever I desired with no problems. Then I turned forty and suddenly experienced intense stomach pain followed by painful gas and bloating after consuming dairy products.

The human body changes. Or more accurately, the body is always in a state of *adjusting* to change. Sometimes these adjustments to change happen so slowly you won't notice them until they've reached a tipping point. Other times, you'll get subtle hints that something is slightly different—like walking just feels better than running. The truth is, these adjustments require you to place attention on what feels good for your body right now, while recognizing your body may feel differently tomorrow.

The human body's messages are subtle. Well, for a while, until they aren't. For the most part the body is designed to operate quite effectively while carrying on your wonderful life. Just imagine if your conscious mind had to remind you to take a breath, blink your eyes, or digest your food. We are incredibly fortunate to live in a body that exquisitely handles countless life-providing activities for us, each and every day. In addition to managing your daily operations, your body is constantly adapting.

For example, your body adapts to the temperature outside, the positions you sit in, your rate of breathing, and detoxification during sleep. Behind the incredible task of supporting life, the body and its systems are working 24/7, each and every day.

All this to say that while the body is accustomed and wired to adapt, it doesn't necessarily choose to adapt only to the "healthy stuff." The body also adapts to absorb and handle the "not so healthy stuff." Simply put, your body puts up with lots of crap. If you eat poorly, you feel poorly. If you choose not to challenge your muscles, they'll decondition. Your body is simply adapting to your choices! This decrease of the body's ability happens slowly and very subtly. Months and years can pass before you realize, "Wow, I'm out of breath walking up these stairs," or "Hmm, I can't bend down comfortably anymore." It's not that your body *decided* to stop being flexible. Along the way, you began to use less of your flexibility. You stopped bending your knees and squatting down to pick up the laundry; you never lay down on the floor anymore. Your body simply adjusts to the demand placed on it.

I simply must remind you: "Use it or lose it" is true for the body.

The decrease of the body's ability to operate with ease happens slowly—almost imperceptibly—until boom, an illness, an injury or a fall gets your attention. Ask yourself, "If I don't take care of my body today, will I notice it tomorrow?" What if you don't take care of yourself for a month, a year, then five years? When will you begin to notice the slow, subtle decline in your health and your movement?

Struggling with Time, Energy and Money

People struggle with not having enough time to take a walk, meditate in the morning, or eat nutritiously. People struggle with not having enough money for the fancy trainer or expensive dietary supplements. And people struggle with not having enough energy to take care of their body in the way they know they "should be", want to be, or the way others are encouraging them to.

I hear you. You are busy. I mean, three kids under the age of five kind of busy. Guess what, I wouldn't expect you to have the time for your body as much as an empty-nester with grown children or someone retired. You have to find what works for you, right now. Life is situational and always in flux, dictating the degree to which you can devote to your body. Maybe you are taking care of an aging parent, or recently accepted a new job promotion.

Life sometimes calls for special circumstances. I'm asking you to make sure your current situation doesn't dictate too far into your future, meaning do what you can when you can, but get honest about when you can refocus back on your healthy body. Too often, transitions (like moving or getting a new job) or situations (like a divorce or aging parents) can derail a person for so long they never return to caring for themselves, ever.

Another thought on time, money and energy: Each day, you make lots of choices, which means you've got time to make choices that align with your healthy desires. Point blank, it takes just as much time to reach for a third glass of wine as it does for a glass of water. If you've got the money to stop into your nearest coffee shop and get a frozen, blended, full-fat coffee drink with whipped cream three times a week, you've got the money for a healthier option. And if you've got the energy to regularly watch more than an hour or so of TV, mindlessly scroll through social media, or spend every Saturday morning shopping, well, you've got time to invest in your body and your health.

Having a relationship with your body may seem like you are adding something to your to-do list. Not necessarily. You are already taking time, energy and money to feed, water, and move your body. So how can you begin to align those choices with your desires and your body's needs?

Getting Stuck in Your Story

Years ago, I was teaching a movement class in a beautiful exposed-brick dance studio in a cultural arts center that decades earlier was a local elementary school. The studio was originally the school's gymnasium. One day, an elegant woman walked in to take a group class. After the 60-minute mindful and soulful dance class, she came up to me in tears. She explained how this building was her elementary school and in this very room, she took "dreaded PE class." She hated PE and recalled how her knees always hurt running in the gym. She began to share with me how she realized after all these years she was still referring to her knees as "bad knees." Even though now her knees rarely gave her any trouble and actually felt quite good, she was stuck in an undeserving story.

One of the biggest problems in getting happy with your body are the long-held, sometimes unconscious beliefs, stories and conclusions that get in the way of your personal wellbeing. It's easy to get caught up in stories about how you can never be the kind of person who eats well. Or you don't deserve to take care of yourselves. Unconscious beliefs can sabotage progress or keep you from ever starting a meaningful journey. As young children, you saw things. You were told things. You picked up on language and verbal assaults from family members, or other influential people in your lives. Your experiences altered your way of being in the world. You learned to protect yourself by creating certainty in your mind and drawing conclusions where you didn't have to question the happenings of life quite so much. Throughout the years, you picked up clues about yourself based on other people's misguided ways of treating you.

Perhaps someone made you feel like you weren't worth giving attention to. Or that you weren't lovable. The most impressionable experiences of your life can continually play out like a running, looped tape, influencing the decisions you make about your body without you even realizing it.

The good news is you can begin a new story, today.

In order to do that, it's valuable to reflect back and recognize where some of these stories and agendas were first created. Bringing your attention to these memories can help you better understand the habit of thinking what you do.

Creating Your Body Biography

We have many feelings and stories about our bodies, our health, and how our bodies operate (like whether they have failed us or not). These stories can be misperceptions that unconsciously create damage throughout our lives. We may not initially be able to recognize where many of these stories originated. Was the story of feeling fat, ugly, slow, lazy etc. our own conclusion, or was it passed down from a peer, loved one, or family member?

Your body's biography is a way to excavate and bring awareness to the habitual stories you tell and retell yourself. Better understanding these moments and the conclusions you drew from them can be an important step in re-creating a meaningful and positive relationship with your body.

A few years back I was working on my relationship with money. Money coach Mikelann Valterra introduced me to Karen McCall's *Money Autobiography*. After working through it, I immediately saw the value in doing this exercise, but geared toward my body. Mikelann writes in her course, *Eleven Steps to Conquering Underearning:* "Before you lay a belief down you must name it. You must be clear what the message was. These old messages may have made sense at one time. Or maybe not. Some messages simply served to keep us in our place. Some messages we inherited were our parents working out their own issues and dealing with their own pain."

Let's begin with some gentle inquiry. Understand your journaling reflects your thoughts and feelings of today, right now. They are useful and yet they can be transformed.

Please find a place of ease, where you can write what you need to say without overanalyzing or overthinking. This process is one of discovery and self-inquiry, not of perfectionism. There is no right, no wrong and no place for judgement. You are writing what you remember and how you feel about those memories. Take your time. You can go through your Body Biography over a series of days or weeks, revisiting it as you wish.

Young Childhood (under 10 years old)

During young childhood it is your family that plays the most significant role in your experiences and stories.

What or who was your greatest influence on you and your outlook on your body?

Was Mom constantly dissatisfied and dieting, or Dad constantly ignoring his health?

What messages, spoken or unspoken, did you receive from family experiences in regards to your body?

Did anyone else in your family–siblings, grandparents–influence your experience, or how you felt about your body?

Consider your young childhood, prior to puberty. Write down one or two memories or stories you have around your body. Include parents, siblings or friends if they were a part of the story.

Adolescence (age 12-17)

Somewhere around the age of 12, at the onset of puberty, friends become a greater influence. Consider yourself between the ages of 12-17, in the midst of puberty but not quite an independently-living adult. Write down one or two memories or stories you have around your body. Include friends, teachers, parents or siblings if they were part of the story.

Do you have any vivid memories or stories that feel significant around peers and friends who may have influenced how you felt about your body?

Do you have a memory or particular instance when you noticed, with the onset of puberty, your body developing?

Did you notice how people reacted toward you and your newly-developed body?

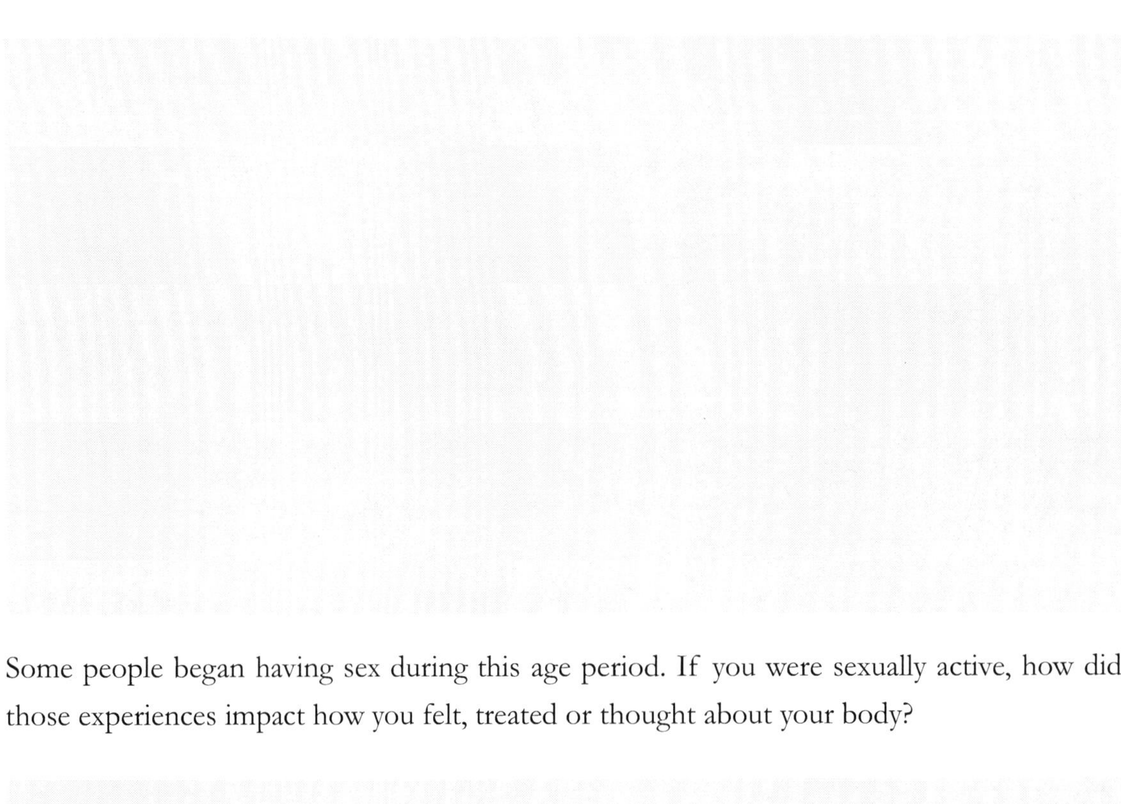

Some people began having sex during this age period. If you were sexually active, how did those experiences impact how you felt, treated or thought about your body?

Young Adulthood (age 18-26)

This is a time period of more independent living. You make your own choices and at times, experience somewhat dramatic feelings and outcomes as a result of those choices. Young adulthood can be a mixed bag of feeling freedom and exploration around your body or feeling devalued or confused about your body.

As you consider your young adulthood years, what strong memories or stories about your body come to mind? And what feels significant about this particular incident/happening?

Whether you went away to college, got married or began working, how did this new life situation affect your body, your health or how you felt about your body?

Adulthood

How do you describe your current stage of life (empty nester, young mother, active senior)?

When it comes to your body, what might be unique about this age and stage of life? For example, child bearing, menopause, professional demands.

Over the last ten years, or time period after young adulthood, what are the significant and influential incidents that have come up surrounding you and your body?

What do you currently believe about your body? You can use the prompt "I believe my body is…"

How long have you felt this way about your body?

What is the current and recurring dialogue between you and your body (I have bad knees, I'm fat, out of shape)?

In a "perfect world" how would you like to feel about your body? Does it feel possible?

Just in case we missed something from the time periods above, what was a potent experience, memory, message or story regarding your body?

Can you remember a time when your body's experience started on a path towards disconnecting? What was the feeling (betrayal, shame, frustration, denial)?

List some situations, stories or memories where you felt healthy or had positive feelings or sensations in regards to your physicality, body or health (strong, fast, steady). What was the scenario and time period?

Connecting the Dots

Being in the space of reflecting on your body's biography, write down a few bullet points you can extract from the stories above. These bullet points are a reflective way of connecting the dots from your upbringing and history to how you live your life with your body now.

For example, one of my stories is my family, particularly my father, teasing me and sometimes being upset with me because as a child, I moved a lot. I was squirmy. I was the child who couldn't sit still. I would lay on the floor, watch TV and still have a leg or bent knee rocking back and forth. I also moved quickly and continue to hear my father's voice saying, "Jill, slow down." I grew up feeling ungraceful. In my zeal to move with my long, awkward arms, I often broke things. My parents reprimanded me for being careless and not paying attention. I grew up feeling like a klutz, even though I continued to run, play tennis against the garage door, ride my bike, and dance in the basement. Over the years, I've come to realize that movement is a blessing to me, not a curse. Movement became my joyful tool for discovering myself over and over again.

My nuggets from childhood:

- being constantly yelled at for moving and breaking things
- feeling awkward and ungraceful
- continuing to move and discovering I was happiest when I was moving, playing or exercising
- feeling most comfortable outdoors, moving and playing or even doing chores
- getting punished and ridiculed for something that I eventually realized wasn't really my fault (breaking things accidentally)

Ask Yourself and Journal...

How can you connect the dots of your body's biography? Which stories from your past continue to shape your thinking today?

SECTION II

Getting to Know You

"People need to know that they have all the tools within themselves. Self-awareness, which means awareness of their body, awareness of their mental space, awareness of their relationships—not only with each other, but with life and the ecosystem."

— Deepak Chopra

CHAPTER 04

Develop a Relationship Mindset

My greatest wish is for you to stop struggling with your body. Nothing breaks my heart more than to think of you hating what I think is one of the most magical creations: your body. I don't want to help you fix your body. And you don't have to fix yourself either. Frankly, no one needs to be telling others how they need to be fixed. If anything, we all could use more understanding, compassion and love for ourselves and our bodies. It is all too common for us to think, "This is how I am broken. Now how do I fix it?" Or, "Just fix it for me so I can go on living my life."

If only bodies could quickly and easily be fixed, like a machine. Replace this bolt. Pull out this part. Fill the tank with oil. But your body isn't a one-dimensional machine, performing a simple task, equipped with a maintenance manual. Your body is an intricate series of systems, independent and interrelated, layered with magical complexities and the unique ability to constantly change and adapt to multiple situations. And amidst all this complexity, the body has one solitary and omnipotent focus, one major purpose which all systems are hardwired to report to—keeping you alive! Yes, your body is singularly dedicated to you. Not your kids. Not your lover. And certainly not your work. Your body is singularly devoted to you, your well-being, your pleasures and your dreams.

I'm going to say it right here: My approach of getting happy with your body usually doesn't address the problems clients first want to address. Classic problems like wanting to lose weight, look better, or exercise more consistently. What I've discovered is that ultimately, clients are unhappy with how their bodies look, perform, or feel, and they are worn out and tired of being so unhappy about it. Naturally, they think, "If I'm unhappy with how my body looks, then I will simply change how my body looks and then I'll be happy with it!" Or, if they don't like the way their body performs, for example they keep injuring their shoulder, then let's fix their shoulder and they'll be done getting injured. Ta-da! Easy-peasy.

Getting happy with your body creates shifts within you, so you can embrace your magnificently devoted body. What kind of shifts? Mindset shifts—so you desire to learn from, live in, and love your body, through all your ages. As you practice getting happy with your body, you begin to understand your body on a different and deeper level, with more attention to detail. You'll find ways to appreciate your body and become deeply grateful for all it does. Your body will become a place of wonderment and you'll learn to approach it with more fascination and less frustration.

When you are living with your body, you no longer have to convince yourself to exercise. You won't feel like you have to go exercise. Instead, you'll cultivate a desire to move your body in ways that challenge it, while feeling good. Dancing, walking, interval training, lifting weights—whatever you decide—become other avenues and opportunities for you to be with your body. Instead of battling your body, you'll begin to listen and respond to your body, moving towards better health and happiness. I want you to discover the benefits of a relationship mindset that will have you understanding, respecting, and appreciating your body.

These clients did:

"You ignited in me a deep and seemingly lasting curiosity and wonderment of the body, of my body. What am I going to discover next?"

"I had a lifelong history of hating exercise and didn't do much of it except to go for an occasional walk or hike with friends. It had always been something I "should" do because my doctor told me I needed to do more of it. I always referred to exercise as the "E" word, like a bad word. Well that changed the day I met you. You helped me to replace that word with "movement."

Embrace Being "With" Your Body

Getting happy with your body, in its simplest form, boils down to a four-letter word: WITH.

What is it like to be *with* your body?

This may seem an odd concept. "What do you mean, be *with* my body? My body is around all the time!" Yes, but how often are you really with your body? Considering your body? Lavishing your body with love and positive attention? Listening to your body's needs and desires? And what about this big question: How often do you consider what it may be like for your body to be living with YOU?

Living with one another—your body and you—is the secret Holy Grail to finally getting happy with your body once and for all.

Does the phrase "have a relationship with your body" leave you scratching your head? No worries, you are in the right place. When people would ask me about my profession, I would naively say, "I help women develop a loving relationship with their body." I noticed people nodding, tipping their heads and saying something like "huh...okay..." A few brave souls would say, "I don't get it, what do you mean by relationship with my body?"

I'll never forget taking a Lyft ride in Phoenix. The driver, Georgina, was a vibrant, middle-aged woman from Chicago. She had a full-time successful career and was new to Phoenix. Driving for Lyft was helping her get acquainted with the city. She was an animated, gregarious driver and we easily started to chat. She asked me what I did for work. "I help women develop a loving relationship with their body," I said. Well, that uncorked a jovial onslaught of questions. I answered her questions the best I could. I talked about reframing her mindset, so she could view her body similarly to other relationships. She could treat her body like she treated others in her life, whether it be a friend, lover, co-worker, or a beloved pet. She could be with her body daily, getting to know her body, learning to listen to her body, and ultimately loving her body, just like those other meaningful people in her life.

"Oh, giiirl, I *never* thought about my s body like *that!* I wish I had known that sooner!"

Relationship is defined as a connection, association, or involvement. *With* is my abbreviated definition for relationship. The definition of the word with is "in relation to." When you are in a relationship *with* someone you ultimately are being with them and they are being *with* you. You are being/living/working in relation to each other. You are, in fact, relating to one another. And so it goes with your body. You have a relationship *with* your body as you spend all day with it—24 x 7 x 365. You are in constant involvement with your body. When your body hurts, so do you. When your body achieves something amazing, so do you. As your body ages, life begins to change for you. Your body has separateness and yet is deeply connected, associated and involved with you, intertwined in a moment-to-moment relationship.

Treat Your Body as an "Other"

Generally, relationships are between two: one and an Other. Not another. I mean "an Other", which is how I'll refer to it from this point forward, capitalizing it like a proper name. Whether it be you and another person or you and something else, you are in several relationships with Others. You have a relationship with your pet. You have a relationship with food. You have a relationship with your car or your smart phone. Anything you come into contact with and interact with, over a period of time, begins to develop a relationship. Because relationships are connections, associations or involvements, whether that be with people, pets or objects.

The relationship with your body can be viewed through a lens like your other relationships. You have relationships with friends, colleagues, and family members. These relationships are likely slightly different from one another. After all, you go to the nightclub with your friends, not your parents. You open up and share your innermost desires and secrets with your closest sibling, not your co-worker. No two relationships are exactly the same. And the one with your body is unique, too. One of the most immediate and inescapable relationships you have is with your body. Obviously, you live in your body, even if you don't pay much attention to it. Your body is your location, your biological suit, which enables your thoughts, feelings and unique experiences a place to dwell. You are always—no matter your level of consciousness—interacting with your body, whether you feel comfortable in it or not.

From the moment you were born, you instantly had a connection to and an involvement with your body.

As part of getting happy with your body, I'm going to ask you to continually view your body as an Other, as *your* Other, similar to a friend, lover or other meaningful person, pet or object in your life. Your body is an essential part of you, complete with its unique individual desires and needs. Your body is an Other that performs specific required duties, like breathing, blinking, etc. Your body also needs the right combination of nutrients, water, rest and activity to handle those duties successfully. Considering and ultimately embracing your body as an Other allows you to ask and reflect, "How am I treating my Other, my body, today (this month, this year, this lifetime)."

Ask Yourself and Journal...

In what ways do you treat your body similarly to your friends and loved ones?

In what ways do you treat your body differently than them?

We cultivate and nurture relationships with those we enjoy and who bring value to us, like supporting us, cheering us up, entertaining us, and showing us love. In what ways does your body bring value to your life?

We are accustomed to considering others' needs. How often do you consider your body's needs and desires?

Create Relationship Touchstones for Your Body

Relationships vary between loving, healthy and valuable, to vacant, disrespectful or even abusive. Many individuals find their relationships leave them disappointed, frustrated or confused. They don't feel heard, seen or valued. Oftentimes in unhappy relationships, the Other doesn't consider your needs and desires. Ultimately, the relationship lacks understanding, respect and appreciation.

When your daily interactions lack these three important touchstones—understanding, respect and appreciation—the entire relationship suffers. When this happens, you may find yourself 1) wanting to avoid the Other, 2) speaking negatively about the Other (to others or in your own head), or 3) acting and responding to the Other in unloving ways.

Have you ever acted these ways with your body? Have you ever wanted to avoid dealing with your body? Spoken negatively about how your body looks or how parts of your body function? And do you ever act or respond to your body in unloving ways?

These questions may be a clue to the relationship you are currently having with your body.

Understand, respect and appreciate are three words that serve as touchstones when re-creating your relationship with your body. They serve as benchmarks for gentle considerations on how to be with your body.

- **Be Understanding** towards your body
- **Have Respect** for your body
- **Be Appreciative** of your body

As often as you can. For as long as you can.

Getting happy with your body means:

- You seek to *understand* your body by listening to its messages.
- You *respect* your body by acknowledging its abilities, qualities and achievements.
- You *appreciate* your body by creating pleasurable experiences for it.

What would it look and feel like to have an understanding, respectful and appreciative relationship with your body?

Let's take a deeper look at our Relationship Touchstones to gain a better understanding of how we can bring them into the relationship with our body.

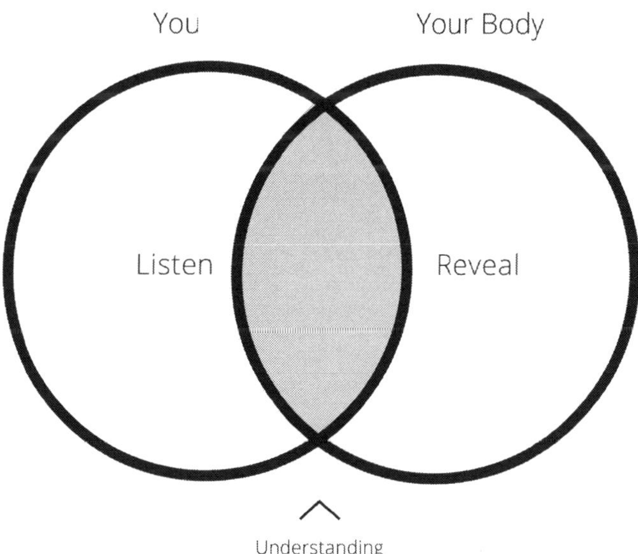

Touchstone One: Understanding

adjective- sympathetically aware of other people's feelings; tolerant and forgiving.

This graphic depicts one revealing while the Other listens. The overlapping combination of both creates an overlap of understanding.

Understanding as an adjective implies how you can respond to an event or a person. You can be sympathetically aware of an Other, whether that person be a friend, a lover or even a stranger. When you cultivate an understanding relationship with an Other, you listen to what the Other reveals to you and respond. In a healthy relationship, you consider the Other's needs and desires and respond accordingly.

Based on the graphic above, consider how your body is the Other, regularly revealing itself to you. Take for example your body revealing it is hungry, tired and cold. You are listening to your body and understanding your body's message. Will you eat? Will you rest? Will you get warm? Approaching your body with understanding may seem straightforward. Yet, how often do you understand what your body is revealing to you, only to ignore its message? For example, do you ever feel hungry but put off eating because you are too busy? Or perhaps you notice your lower back is starting to hurt, but continue to work in the garden, despite your body's soreness? As part of getting happy with your body, you'll practice becoming more aware of the messages your body is revealing to you and how to respond to them with understanding.

Consider your body. If you raised your level of understanding for your body, would you treat it differently? How could understanding your body change your life?

Touchstone Two: Respect

noun- a feeling of deep admiration for someone or something, elicited by their abilities, qualities, or achievements.

This word can carry quite a charge. Today we hear of people demanding "respect." In the definition above, respect is "earned by abilities, qualities or achievements." So, I ask you, do you respect your body? Do you carry a feeling of deep admiration for your body based on its abilities, qualities or achievements? Every single time I study the human body, my level of respect for my body skyrockets. When I learn about my body's daily achievements to keep me alive and consider the abilities it affords me, I am in awe of what a remarkable, living system the body is.

Consider a person you deeply respect. Why do you respect them? What is it they do to earn your respect? And how do you treat them based on your respect for them?

Now consider your body. If you raised the level of respect for your body, would you treat it differently? How could respecting your body change your life?

Touchstone Three: Appreciate

verb- to recognize the full worth of.

Full. Worth.

Enough said.

Think of things and people in your life that you appreciate. You may appreciate your job or career. You may appreciate your education. You may appreciate how your spouse, friend, or partner helps you. You may appreciate how your pet greets you each morning. They provide value in your life and you recognize their worth. Have you considered what your body is worth to you and what value it brings to your life?

If you raised the level of appreciation for your body, would you treat it differently? How could appreciating your body change your life?

Develop Your Own Touchstones

You are welcome to use the Getting Happy with Your Body Relationship Touchstones to understand, respect and appreciate your body, or you may want to create your own touchstones. What touchstone words or phrases best describe the qualities you want to foster between you and your body? Reflect and write what bubbles up from your intuitive guidance. No need to overthink these words. Plus, you may end up fine-tuning the statements as time goes on. For now, simply jot down a few touchstones to describe the relationship you desire with your body (for example: joy, self-acceptance, love, forgiveness, and pleasure).

Consider Likes, Dislikes, Abilities and Limitations

With friends and family, people grow closer to one another by listening to one another, considering each other's needs, and responding lovingly to those needs, while in turn, revealing their own needs. Close relationships develop when there is honesty and a willingness to communicate about needs, desires, dreams, abilities and limitations. For example, if you are afraid of heights (a limitation), your best friend is not likely to drag you out rock climbing and force you to look over a rock ledge to the ground below. If you physically are unable to run 26 miles, or you hate the idea of running, your partner is not likely to sign you up to run a marathon. If you are allergic to nuts, your mother is not likely to add nuts to your favorite birthday cake.

A big part of being in a healthy relationship with an Other is understanding, respecting and appreciating one another's likes, dislikes, abilities and limitations. And we can be this way with our body, too. Can't we? Have you considered your body's likes, dislikes, abilities or limitations, as if you were considering a friend's? Do you lovingly respond to your body when it shares with you what it needs? Or do you bully your body with choices that wear your body down.

Consider Your Body

Write what you currently know about your body's likes, dislikes, abilities and limitations.

A Message from your Body

Hello Dear One,

I'm the voice of the human body. Your body. Created by male and female bodies and the body of your ancestors. I am the body of those you love and those you have yet to love.

I am flesh, bone, blood, oxygen, tissue and energy—I am mostly liquid and space that welcomes your soul and partners with your mind and emotions to create You. Ideally, together in collaboration, we journey through this present life, experiencing the here and now, making memories and history.

Even as I carry your history and past in me, I, your body, live in the now. In my present-moment state, I receive and coordinate your desires, your fears, your thoughts and actions. Breathe into me and my 75 trillion cells.

I, your body, am devoted and dedicated to a single use or purpose. I am devoted to you. Breathe and trust that every single moment of the day I am here, serving you. Following your lead. Reflecting your choices.

I, the universal human body, am designed to move. I am happiest creating force and then relaxing. I respond best to moving in a variety of ways and directions.

I, your body, am an exquisite piece of art created from single cells that formed bone, muscle, tissue and liquids to create this moveable home enabling you to carry forth with your personal desires. As a physical form, in the now moment, I am greatly and undeniably influenced by how you choose to live now and also relive your past. Your personality, thoughts and feelings have great impact on my sustainability, my function and how I appear in the world.

With you, our greatest moments are of homeostasis—perfect harmony—when all, body, mind, and emotions align with your soul's desire to live in this moment. Smell the now. Touch the now. Hear the now. Taste the now. And see the now. To experience me fully in your life, you must live in the now. This is one of my greatest values. I bring you into presence.

Dear one, know that I, your body, am at your service. My mission is always to create balance, health and healing as I remain dedicated to you.

I accept your reverence.

I accept your honor.

I forgive you for the times when you've been unkind to me.

I humbly apologize for the times when you've felt betrayed by me.

I ask only that you open yourself to receive my subtle and not-so-subtle messages of both pain and pleasure, so we can partner in living fully.

Let us discover and love one another.

Forever yours,

Your Body

CHAPTER 05

Examine Other Parts of You

Getting happy with your body is like flipping on a light switch in the dark. Need to see if the dog is chewing on your shoe? Flip on the light switch. Wondering where you left your favorite jacket? Go to the closet and flip on the light switch. When you want to see and find something in an area that is dark, you need light. And so it is when discovering your connection to your body. But sometimes getting in touch with your body feels like fumbling around in a dark room, not realizing a light switch is within reach. And let's be honest, fumbling around in the dark is uncomfortable. For some it's downright scary. When I was a little girl, my older sister often coaxed me to walk her down the long hallway to our bedrooms because she was afraid of the dark. She'd grab my hand and we would scurry down the hall together in our nightgowns until she switched on her bedroom light. She needed a buddy to go through the dark and find the switch. Throughout this book, I'm going to be your buddy on this journey "down the hall," helping you find the light switch to discovering your body.

In my 25 years of working with women who are unhappy about how their bodies look, perform or feel, I've had the honor of helping them flip the switch and find their bodies. With the simple suggestion to "take a breath, clear your mind and drop in to your body," I'd watch the room get still as they shifted their attention away from the outside world and redirected their energy towards their inside world, their body. They were IN their body. In this being-ness, they experienced feeling serenely content to ecstatic. Afterwards, through moist, smiling eyes they'd often share with me how during the experience they felt "at home." Yes, our bodies truly are our physical homes, where we inhabit and exist in the here and now.

I am continually surprised at how quickly people reconnect to their bodies when given the space, time and encouragement to do so. In these moments, it all seems so simple. What do these clients do? Two things: first, they place their attention on their body, and second, they let go of anything in the way of doing that.

Meet Your Others: Mind, Emotions, Spirit, and Body

In the previous chapter, we talked about the body as an "Other," which you cultivate a relationship with. Well, if your body is one part of you, what about your mind, emotions, and spirit? Couldn't these unique aspects of yourselves also be considered "others"? They certainly each have their own unique functions that help you live out your life each and every day.

- Your Mind is the mental part of you where you engage in thinking, computing, strategizing, and imagining.

- Your Emotions are the feeling part of you where you engage in a range of feelings from love to fear.

- Your Spirit is an indescribable and personal part of you where you engage in having unique experiences.

- Your Body is the physical part of you, where you sense your current physical environment.

If the room to your body seems dark and uninhabited, then where are you living? Which "Other" are you engaging most of the time? Are you spending the majority of your time in your mind, filled with thinking, planning and imagining? What about your emotions? Are you overwhelmed with feelings of joy (I hope!), concern, or irritation? More now than ever, our lives seem to revolve around thinking and feeling, partly due to the fact we have so many physical conveniences all that's left is to engage our mind. I believe humans love to do. Our body is designed to move. We are born to create, invent, fix problems, and improve our surroundings. For centuries, we've used a combination of our minds and bodies to do so. Previous generations had the benefit of using their minds to imagine, and then using their bodies to fulfill that creation. Today, many of us experience a different scenario. We imagine and invent solutions and improvements, only to sit at our desk, our bodies nearly asleep with inactivity, to materialize those creations.

When you live in an overactive mind, it is difficult to be in your body. When you live in your body, it is less likely you'll be overactive with your mind.

This chapter is to help you recognize which Others you rely on as well as discover if you leave your body in the dark.

Your Mind…What are You Thinking?

Getting happy with your body consists of living in, understanding and enjoying your body. How can this happen if you are consistently placing your attention elsewhere? For example, a luxurious massage is certainly a less enjoyable experience if you are constantly distracted by background noise or thinking about a worrisome work situation. Sure, you may get the massage but because you were elsewhere with your mind, you've likely missed out on receiving all the pleasant physical sensations of the massage.

Placing your attention elsewhere can sweep you away from what you are actually experiencing physically. I'm not saying this is always a bad thing. Daydreaming, imagining, considering, analyzing, and remembering are all powerful tools of the mind and serve you in countless ways. However, if you struggle with placing your attention on your body, usually repetitive and pronounced mind activity is distracting you away from it. Thankfully, the more frequently you practice getting in your body, the more your monkey mind will ease. And likewise, when you ease your monkey mind, you will be more able to drop into your body.

What happens when I ask you to flip your light switch and use your mind to bring your attention to your body? Let's give it a try.

Take a breath. Allow your body to relax with each exhale. Quiet your mind and direct your attention inwards to your body. Imagine your entire body illuminated. Close your eyes and stop reading for 60 seconds.

Don't worry, I'll be here when you are done.

How'd that feel? How do *you* feel? Could you get a sense of dimming the activity of your mind and increasing the attention towards your body? Was there a point when your mind came barging in on your experience? Did you begin to get a little antsy, maybe wondering "what am I *doing* here"? All of those unique and awkward sensations are perfectly natural because what you were doing was *being with your body.*

Your mind is not the enemy of your body. In fact, you need your mind to be with your body. However, do you find you use your mind to constantly think about other things, while giving your body very little attention? Instead, what if you partnered with your mind and crafted a healthier, more balanced use of your mind's energy in order to stay in touch with your body. If you want to understand, respect and appreciate your body, the best place to start is by directing your mind's attention towards your body. So often we want to know our body better, yet we are placing our attention elsewhere. How often do you hear yourself say (whether to someone else or yourself):

"Let me think about that."

"Let me consider that."

"I need to plan, analyze or pro-con-pro that." One of the biggest challenges may be quieting your mind's tendency for ongoing chatter long enough to be with your body.

Ask Yourself and Journal...

How active is your mind? Are you *always* thinking? Or better yet, is there ever a time you aren't thinking *so much*?

Do you feel like there is so much static going on in your head that every message from your body is drowned out?

Do you find yourself with a single thought you simply can't let go of? If so, what thought is it?

Do you churn scenarios in your head, over and over? Again, write the scenario down.

Your Emotions...What are You Feeling?

When my kids were toddlers, on the verge of a tantrum, I would ask them if they were having "big feelings." Their feelings felt overwhelming, and at that age they lacked the verbal tools to express themselves. As adults, we have a larger vocabulary to describe our feelings and express ourselves more clearly. But do we do it? How often do we ask ourselves, "Is this the emotion I'm truly feeling"? It is easy to stick with the basic, highly popular emotions: I feel bummed, depressed, sad, happy, excited, loved, frustrated, angry, pissed, scared, tired. Tired. I had to name it twice, because I hear it so often.

What are your go-to labels for describing how you feel?

Do you often say, "I'm tired"? It begs the question—tired of what? Tired where? In your body, physically? In your mind, mentally? Or in your spirit, an indescribable way of being tired? We use words to describe how we think we're feeling, but are we being specific enough to fully share what we are feeling?

Understanding your feelings is a vital piece of getting happy with your body. Why? Because your emotional state influences your actions and how you treat your body.

What do you do when you are feeling stressed? Do you eat sweets? When you are feeling unhappy do you consume alcohol? If you are feeling anxious what choice do you make to cope with your anxiousness? Take a sleep aid? Meditate?

Keep in mind, your emotions have a range of intensity, and being accurate in describing them entails understanding which degree of a certain emotion you are feeling. For example:

- You can be slightly concerned, afraid, or at worst, terrified. Feeling concerned is certainly different than feeling absolutely terrified.
- You can be mildly content, happy, or completely ecstatic. Try on feeling content right now. Now, what if you were to switch to being ecstatic? Different, huh?
- You can be a little annoyed, pretty angry, or wildly furious. Have you ever felt yourself go from being irate to wildly furious? Yup, certainly a range of emotional intensity.

How you feel about yourself and your situations fuels your choices. And many times, those choices do not align well with a healthy, happy body. Let's not overlook that happy emotions can prompt choices, too. Food, drink, and dance are all parts of a wonderful, joyful celebration. I'm not suggesting you change how you cope with your emotions or celebrate life events. At this point, I am suggesting you become aware of your emotions and specific feelings you are experiencing.

Your mind thinks. Your emotions feel. You choose and your body handles it.

Ask Yourself and Journal...

Take some time throughout the day for the next few days to observe how often you use the same words to describe what you are feeling, whether you are talking to yourself or someone else. Write them down here as your "go-to emotional labels."

The Emotion Wheel

Then ask yourself if these words are truly describing how you are feeling? If you can, catch yourself the moment you say (I'm ___pissed, happy, tired) and assess how accurately and precisely you're describing your current feelings. Can you be even more descriptive with the type and intensity of emotion you are feeling? Use the emotional wheel above to help you get started.

Your Spirit (Soul, Essence, Guide)…What Does it Mean to You?

This Other part of us goes by many names and is deeply personal to many people. Instead of a steadfast name we all agree on, I'll leave it up to you. What do you call the Other part of you that is not your emotions, your mind or your body? The place where you feel a knowingness and connection you can't quite explain. For some, spirit comes from outside themselves and is something they connect to for comfort and guidance. For others, the soul is within, a deep place coded to them. Some people believe they have a soul and they connect to spirit. My point here is we all have something indescribably unique and specific to us that is not our emotions, not our body and not our mind. This uniqueness can provide us with insight, wisdom and knowingness beyond what we've formally learned. Spirit-Soul-Essence-Guide—whatever you name it, I recognize its importance in life, though I will not be addressing it as much as the others (mind, emotions, body) in this book. For our purposes, I draw your attention to its existence as an Other. I encourage you to recognize the moments where you aren't thinking or feeling, yet somehow are deeply guided with a sense of knowingness, in a way that is unique to you.

Ask Yourself and Journal…

What word best describes this uniqueness for you? How do you connect to it?

Ask Yourself and Journal...

What is your general state of being when you feel connected to it?

How big a part does this particular aspect of yourself play in your life?

Your Body: What are You Physically Experiencing?

Your body brings you physically into the world. More than your mind or emotions, your body lives in the present moment, reporting its current experience. I will be talking a lot more about how your body communicates with you further in the book. For now, consider this—your mind and emotions speak to you in a language you are accustomed to hearing and clearly understand. You know—the voice you hear in your head. Well, your body communicates too, but in a language all its own. This language is one of physical sensation, where you feel something in your physical body and then your brain decodes the sensation in order to understand what that sensation means.

We have a vocabulary for many sensations; for example: hot and cold for temperature, smooth and sticky for touch, or heavy and light for pressure. But some messages the body sends feel new or different to us, making them more difficult to decode and even more difficult to understand what we should do to help ourselves when we receive them.

We'll address this specifically in Section Three, as you'll learn to notice and sense your body so you can make choices that align with your body's desires and needs.

What physical sensations do you most notice in your body? Pain, stiffness, warmth, comfort? Where in your body do you notice them?

Are you aware of any physical sensations right now? Where are they in your body?

The Difference Between Mind, Emotions and Body

One big difference between the mind, emotions and body is their ability to time travel. The mind can recall past events, conjure up feelings, and relive emotions. For example, thinking back on the experience of having a baby, I can use my mind to remember the hospital room, the people there, and parts of conversations. Thinking of the experience nostalgically brings me feelings of contentment. I feel happy going back in time thinking about the event. My mind has created a movie of memories in my head, and emotions and feelings are part of the soundtrack. Obviously, the birth of a child is quite vivid; I can get caught up in my memories and nearly feel like I'm there all over again. Except my body is still here in the present moment. I do not have the physical discomfort of labor that I had in the hospital on that day. I might be able to recall the discomfort or pain, but my body is not physically experiencing it right now. So, while the mind and emotions can take a trip back in time, in most cases, the physical body doesn't go with them.

Time travel also happens when you think about the future. Thinking ahead to the future is a way of projecting what may happen. On the positive side, you can engage your mind and imagine your future. This can conjure up feelings of hope and excitement, or on the flip side, these thoughts might make you feel more anxious or fearful.

"If you are depressed, you are living in the past. If you are anxious, you are living in the future. If you are at peace, you are living in the present." —Lao Tzu, Mystic Philosopher of Ancient China

You can choose how to use your mind to travel. Will you think about the future with fear and worry? Or can you imagine a better scenario? When you reflect on the past, do you easily dredge up scenarios where you were unhappy? Becoming more consciously aware of your mind and emotions will allow you to notice their tendencies. And then you can begin to discern how to use your mind to your benefit. Why is all this important? Because in order to connect to your body, you'll want to track what your mind and emotions are saying to you.

I mention this now because as you move forward with getting happy with your body, you'll begin to see how your mind and emotions can influence how you treat your body. For example, many of us eat when we are sad. Or we may ignore our lower back pain because we are so lost in our latest work project. If your mind and emotions are constantly somewhere else, they can't be paying attention to your body. In order to develop a healthy relationship with your body, practice hanging out with your body, just like a friend you are getting to know better. With practice, you can harness the mind and emotions to build the relationship you want with your body. You can teach yourself to flip the light switch and be present with your body.

Ask Yourself and Journal...

Consider which of the Others are dominating your life? Is it your mind, body, emotions or spirit?

Are you aware of any mental and/or emotional traps that keep you reliving the past? If so, what are they?

How often do you place your attention on what you are doing and experiencing right now?

CHAPTER 06

Recognize Your Body Archetype

Now that you've learned about your mind, emotions and body as separate Others, this chapter will share how ingrained recurring thoughts, feelings and behaviors can form Body Archetypes that can hinder us from a loving relationship with our body.

Janet had been in a lot of pain over the last two years. She'd experimented with shifting her diet, changing her exercise program, becoming more aware of her emotions, and doing her best to decrease her stress. She came to me to explore yet another modality that might help her get out of her chronic pain. I admired her for continuing to explore ways to help herself feel better. When she walked in, I could tell right away she was in pain. I have found over the years there is an energetic quality that surrounds a person in chronic pain. Her movements were deliberate and limited. She seemed to hold herself close to her body. She smiled with her mouth but her eyes told a different story. I've come to notice people in pain tend to clench. Sometimes I see it around their eyes, mouth, or in Janet's case, her hands—arms hanging dead-like by her side with her hands in tight fists; the result of having to "grin and bear it."

I worked with Janet for a few hours. Some of my go-to mindfulness work didn't seem helpful. Just noticing her body was difficult for her. The act of sensing was too much—too many messages of discomfort flooding her way. Intuitively, I asked her to move a part of her body that didn't hurt. I encouraged her to focus her mind on the movement in that body part and the sensation of being pain-free. She chose to move her forearms in a gently flowing sway. Eventually, she began to meander through the studio space in a soft, gliding way. She told me the movement in that part of her body felt good, new and unusual. I was pleased to have suggested a possible opening—to find movements that her body could do, pain-free, to help her sense, enjoy and absorb that pleasurable sensation. Upon my suggestions she replied, "That exercise was interesting, but I just want this pain to go away so I can stop dealing with my body and get on with my life, like before."

After that appointment, I came home and wrote my thoughts and revelations about Body Archetypes. Body Archetypes represent how our mind and emotions influence us to treat our body. Being stuck in a certain way of thinking causes us to habitually approach our relationship with our body. For Janet, even though she had experienced something new that felt good, her mind was only allowing a quick-fix option. Her habitual way of being with her body and need to "fix it fast" was keeping her from a new approach and limiting her possibility of becoming more pain-free.

It happens so slowly we hardly notice it—entrenchment. We become so deeply accustomed to living a certain way, we cannot imagine, see or feel our way out. The long-term discomfort we've been experiencing becomes known and therefore, in a strange way, comfortable and predictable.

Archetypes are described as an original pattern or model from which all things of the same kind are copied or based. In Jungian psychology, archetypes represent a collective inherited unconscious idea or pattern of thought.

As you read the various Body Archetypes, do your best to contain your mind's tendency to judge. Instead, I invite you to approach yourself with understanding, compassion and curiosity. By reflecting on the Body Biography exercise from Chapter Three, you may find some connections between your upbringing and social history to certain Body Archetypes that resonate with you.

The Body Bully Archetype

- Has a "just do it" attitude
- Ignores body sensations/messages

The Body Bully does what *they* want without much consideration for their body. The body is simply a vehicle for their own wants and desires. The Body Bully is willing to suffer the consequences of treating their body without consideration. They literally bully their body into doing, performing or moving in the way the ego wants and demands. The Body Bully often has a severe "pay to play" or "just do it" attitude. Typically, injuries are nuisances that are given little attention. There are no excuses once the ego has set its sights on something. The Body Bully shows little concern for how this behavior might affect their body in the future.

The Body Bully benefits from:

In a life or death situation, the Body Bully archetype can be a lifesaver. However, to operate in this archetype day in and day out can have serious physical and emotional ramifications. The Body Bully can benefit from a sense of recognizing that the body does in fact have limitations. At some point, the body will not be able to tolerate certain activity levels, eating habits or abuses. There is a tipping point somewhere in the future. Awareness is needed. You can in fact balance "going for it" with self-care, understanding and awareness. As a Body Bully, you will benefit greatly from simply taking moments to recognize how and when you are bullying your body. Notice bullying thoughts. Consider taking on a more adaptive approach where you can respond to the needs of your body versus purposefully pushing beyond them. Begin to develop the skills to appreciate what your body is doing and how your body is handling your demands.

The Body Blamer Archetype

- Sees the body as defective and blames it
- Harbors anger or pity towards the body

This archetype blames the body for aches and pains. They are angry at the situation with their body, and perhaps frustrated with their lack of control over their body. The Body Blamer emotionally blames the body for what they aren't getting to do or achieve. They allow their body, and the blame they have for it, to stop them from their happiness or fulfillment. This archetype also leads to a sense of feeling powerless. "My body is doing this to me, so therefore I can (or cannot) do this." Their blame can become aggressive. Pity is their passiveness.

The Body Blamer benefits from:

It's helpful for the Body Blamer to recognize their body actually has a very limited ability to create mistreatment. The body doesn't have the mindset to antagonize you or be vengeful. The body is often under attack on a cellular level throughout the day. Most of the time it wins. However, at times the fight is greater than it can handle, and the body gets sick or injured. Symptoms and situations are often the result of the body doing its best to survive and return to homeostasis, always seeking natural balance. The body is a system that continually responds to its environment in order to maintain survival.

Consider what your actions and choices may be in contributing to your body's response. Take ownership for what is yours and cultivate awareness for what is out of your control. Recognize that you ultimately choose how to experience your body. Consider refocusing and learning about the ways your body is healing and performing amidst your choices and demands. Consider developing fascination (versus frustration) around what your body is in fact doing for you all day long.

The Body Oblivious/Body Archetype

- Is out of touch with their body
- Thinks about their body as a completely new concept

The Body Oblivious/Body Innocent archetype is completely clueless about their body. Their answer is always "I don't know," or "I never thought about that or noticed that." They do not consider their body, but not because they are bullying it. They operate as if they haven't met their body and rarely acknowledge they are presently living in a body. For the Body Innocent, everything with the body is brand new information, as if a surprise, experienced for the first time.

The Body Oblivious/Innocent benefits from:

If you can identify with the Body Oblivious/Innocent, take baby steps to improve your awareness and connection to your body. One tip: upon waking, before jumping out of bed, move your joints and check in with how each part of your body is feeling. Simply pay attention to what you sense when you move your body parts. Another tip: designate specific times of the day to check in with your body and sense it throughout the day. Maybe it is simply placing your attention on your body when you use the bathroom to brush your teeth in the morning.

The Perpetually Distracted Archetype

- Chooses to escape their body
- Consistently and constantly places attention elsewhere

Many of us fall into this category where we place our attention everywhere but on our body. For the Perpetually Distracted, that is all they choose to do. You'll notice the Perpetually Distracted because they are often 1) listening to an audio book while they walk 2) talking on the phone to "multitask" 3) watching TV on their exercise bike or 4) eating lunch while reading, to name a few examples. They are in a state of distraction from their body and create ways to escape having to pay attention to it. The Perpetually Distracted may actually sense their body yet choose to, on some level, ignore their body. This can come from a host of reasons, like past abuses or hardships. Though the Perpetually Distracted may in fact exercise or eat healthfully, they still live in a state of thinking about something else, and avoid paying attention to their body by placing their attention on almost anything else.

The Perpetually Distracted benefits from:

The simple but powerful act of slowing down, placing your attention on your body and body sensations is helpful for the Perpetually Distracted archetype. Catching yourself in a state of distraction is key. Ask yourself where or what you are placing your attention on now. Is your attention always on other people, your emotions, or the latest drama? Are you focused on external devices like music, television, books or magazines? Once you notice the habits that distract you, you can take focused steps to bring your attention to your body and learn from the messages your body is communicating to you.

The Body Fixer Archetype

- Has a "Fix me, I'm broken" attitude
- Discourages easily and moves on to the next miracle cure

The Body Fixer has a fascination with the next bright and shiny thing that will *fix* them and *their body*. Their motivation is to finally fix their body with the latest trainer, diet or type of exercise. They love the sense of energy that starting something new gives them and the hope that this latest new thing is IT. The serial Body Fixer constantly views their body as something to fix and frequently seeks or purchases something outside themselves to help with their "problematic" body. However, they don't usually commit for very long and become discouraged easily if things don't work out. This can lead to accusing their body of being broken or the failure of their latest shiny new thing they just invested in.

The Serial Body Fixer benefits from:

Awareness and tough questions are at the core for the Body Fixer. Ask yourself: do you enjoy learning what you are learning or are you enjoying experiencing the rush that this may be the one thing to *finally* help you? Is the thought, "THIS. IS. IT!" running excitedly through your mind? Pay attention to the dialogue playing in your mind around your next fix.

Also notice if the fix is always outside yourself. Another trainer, another approach, another diet. You would benefit from well-earned patience, commitment and accountability. Put yourself in a position where you are accountable to yourself (or a supportive friend) and notice when you are, yet again, investing in another new fix instead of learning about yourself and the needs of your body.

The Body Annoyed Archetype

- Feels inconvenienced by their body all the time
- Complains about their body at the slightest inconvenience

The Body Annoyed is similar to the Body Bully but doesn't push the body as hard or beyond its limits. The Body Annoyed hears the body, and may even make choices for the body's comfort and safety; AND they are incredibly annoyed to have to do that, to be inconvenienced by their forever-broken and burdensome body. It could be the inconvenience that annoys them. It could be that they are annoyed by their waning capabilities. Generally, they are annoyed with, angry at, or complaining about their body. The Body Annoyed complains more than blames. Usually the Body Annoyed has a lot on their plate. They have perfectionist tendencies and are upset by not living up to them—and annoyed about having to submit to their body's imperfections.

The Body Annoyed benefits from:

Adding pleasure into the life of the Body Annoyed is key. Has life become one big grind? Is there any connection to pleasure, specifically for the senses—sight, taste, touch, sound, and smell? Indulge your senses. Give yourself some space and time for you and your life to become more "sense-U-all." Allow for a sense of indulgence that brings you back into the pleasures of your body. Slowly savor your favorite food. Bathe your skin in silky bath oils or bath salts. Explore essential oils. Pleasure will lead to relaxation. And relaxation can open the door to the path of body gratitude.

The Body as Betrayer Archetype

- Feels their body has betrayed them
- Holds a grudge against their body

When people feel a strong sense that their body is betraying them, they have the archetype of Body as Betrayer. This archetype usually comes into play when a person has been experiencing an illness or long-standing injury. I can certainly understand how someone suffering from a painful injury or illness can have feelings of betrayal. "How can my body do this to me? I've done everything right!" When people feel betrayed by their body, they are holding the belief that the body is doing wrong or getting back at them. It is important to understand the body doesn't really have an opinion. The body, as a response mechanism, is not spiteful or vengeful. The body does have physical reactions, and most of the time those reactions are in response to some kind of behavior or choice from the body's operator (you and me). And there are times when mystery comes into play; the unexplained, like DNA, heredity, or unseen environmental impacts. There are times when illness or even injuries don't necessarily make sense. With all we know about the body, there is a universe of the unknown yet to be discovered.

The Body as Betrayer benefits from:

Forgiveness is key. Even if your body's performance, health and wellbeing is not reflecting all you've done to take care of it, you'll benefit greatly from forgiveness. Without forgiving your body for its best attempts, you only continue to suffer from blame, anger and disappointment. That is no way to live for yourself or in your body. And though the symptoms you are experiencing may in fact not make any sense and may be incredibly unfair, keep in mind the body is still doing its best to be healthy and well. The body is always striving for the best survival and utmost safety, even though messages can sometimes get confused. In situations when you feel betrayed by your body due to chronic illness or injury, begin to explore the avenue of forgiveness, just as you would forgive a young child or pet. Embarking on unconditional love can create miracles in how you go about living day to day.

Archetypes: One or a Mixed Bag?

None of these fit just right? Great! This exercise is not designed to fit you and how you treat your body into some tidy little box of characteristics. Instead, this chapter is designed to heighten your sensitivity and awareness to how you could possibly be treating your body in a way that keeps you from developing a loving, meaningful and cohesive relationship between you and your body.

Part of developing a relationship with your body is observing what you bring to the relationship. If you show up with your body as "the bully," what outcome does that create? Imagine showing up more compassionately with your body. That compassion is like a gift you bring to your body. How would your body react differently if you treated it with more compassion? Could you heal from a chronic, nagging injury? Would you finally stop beating yourself up over those five extra pounds?

Ask Yourself and Journal...

Which archetype(s) resonate with you? Describe how you normally react to your body.

Describe scenarios where the archetype shows up, like at work, with a loved one, or at the gym.

How is your predominant archetype serving you and your relationship with your body?

Does your archetype's habitual thinking and behavior contribute to your overall suffering? If so, how?

What would your day or your life be like without the presence of the archetype?

Which of the beneficial tools would you like to engage more often and in what scenarios?

SECTION III

Getting to Know Your Body

"Awareness is realizing that our life could always be better. Growth is doing what it takes to make it better."

—Danielle LaPorte

INTRODUCTION

The Be with your Body Practice

Getting happy with your body is about fostering and nurturing a relationship with your body that is similar to building any other relationship that is meaningful and important to you. Take a moment to consider the people in your life whom you enjoy and love. Upon first meeting them you looked them in the eye, smiled, and introduced yourself. In order to learn more about them and ultimately get to know them, you listened to them. And lastly, with each enjoyable interaction, you chose to develop a relationship with them. Building a relationship doesn't happen overnight and isn't always simple, but ultimately having people we enjoy and love in our life is very rewarding.

Now I'd like to introduce you to a similar process, one that will guide you back to your body and create the relationship with your body you've always wanted—a happy one!

The truth is, many of us have spent too much time ignoring our body, cutting ourselves off from the neck down as if the rest of our body is either an inconvenience, a disappointment, or simply nothing at all—vacant. Yet we are looking for a richer existence, one that goes beyond simply operating from only our thoughts or emotions. We are looking for day-to-day experiences where we can feel whole. We yearn for what's missing—being with our body.

As we reclaim our rightful place with our body, we gain a trusted ally that reminds and enables us to live in the present moment, right here and right now. Why is that important? Because life as a human being is best experienced in the richness of the current moment. You can think about the past or the future and cry, wail, grieve, rejoice and celebrate, all with the knowingness that your body will be holding you to the honest reality of the current moment.

You may feel anxious, but your body reveals, in this moment, you are safe. You may think you need to worry about next week, and your body reveals, in this moment, all is well. You may be harboring resentment, and your body reveals, in this moment, you are unburdened. When you live with your body, you become acutely connected to right now, and usually right now is more comforting than what your mind or emotions are presenting to you.

Your body can help you become more mentally and emotionally balanced, too.

One notable experience for me came after my divorce. I was feeling deep grief and sadness, but also relief and optimism. I was, as can be expected, an emotional mess. One morning, with the kids at their dad's, I could feel myself emotionally unraveling. I laid down on the carpet. I knew what was coming. I could sense in my body the waves of grief barely being held back by my thin wall of resistance. Surrendering, the floodgates opened and my tears flowed. I sobbed, wailed, and released the feelings in my heart. As my body physically released, so did those pent up emotions.

After a while, my tears ran dry and my body felt relaxed. I was shocked by how strangely different I now felt: emotionally at peace and physically centered. Being with my body, and allowing my emotions to flow through it, enabled me to let go of the past and eventually return to the present moment. This experience allowed me a new freedom where I was no longer immediately burdened with the emotions bottled up inside me.

Being with your body is profound, and at the same time, relatively simple. It has a soothing effect. Connecting with your body is a form of meditation, partly because it brings a departure away from your overactive mind. Perhaps you've already experienced the benefits if you've ever cleared your mind by going for a walk, or felt more at peace after taking a bike ride. Maybe you've noticed how your mood improves after you work out. Or perhaps you've lifted your energy with a simple stretch or dance break.

When you live with your body, you'll begin to notice the physical benefits of your choices.

And you'll be more apt to make choices that benefit your health and wellbeing.

Two years ago, I had a lower back injury. An area of my spine that once was a subtle nuisance all of a sudden became debilitating. I had never experienced such pain with just the slightest movement. I can still remember being in bed, and how even the weight of the bed sheet was painful. Very scary. Thankfully, over time, my body healed. Throughout my recovery, I constantly relied on the process of being with my body to check in and sense what helped it feel better. Two healthy years later, I still check in regularly with my spine. I recently noticed that sitting in my comfy sofa irritated my spine. If I lay on the floor to watch TV, my back felt great. But if I reclined on the sofa, the previously injured area of my spine would become sore. So now I enjoy lying on the floor or limiting the amount of time I'm on the sofa. This small adjustment keeps my body happy and keeps me feeling pain-free.

Nothing earth shattering, huh?

But what if I didn't listen to my body? What if I didn't notice the sofa made my back worse. Or if I simply continued to do so, and simply went along with the pain, thinking I didn't have any other choices? How often do you put yourself (and your body) in positions of suffering because you fail to notice and sense your body? Or if you do sense your body and physically feel discomfort, do you ignore it—until it gets worse?

Personally, I'd rather struggle and suffer less, and instead do what it takes to keep my body happy.

Recently, a friend told me she had plantar fasciitis, an inflammation of the tissue along the sole of the foot. This overuse injury is relatively common with people who frequently run or stand on their feet. I asked her what she was doing to help it feel better. She told me, "Nothing. I'm just hoping it goes away." What do you think the chances are of it "just going away"? If she continues to do nothing differently, what do you think the chances of it becoming more debilitating are? By being with her body and listening to what makes her foot feel worse and choosing actions that make it feel better, she could avoid worsening the condition, thus helping her body heal faster. She could struggle and suffer less—and so could her body.

On your last leg of this journey towards getting happy with your body you'll learn how to turn towards your body and be with it. You'll practice letting your mind rest so you can experience what is occurring on a physical level. You will engage with your body, allowing you to receive profound information you didn't know had been available to you all along. In order to get there, though, it'll take a little practice. The *Be with your Body Practice* has three simple steps. Each step stands alone as an individual practice, and becomes even more powerful when practiced together.

Meet Your Body, Listen to Your Body and Choose for Your Body

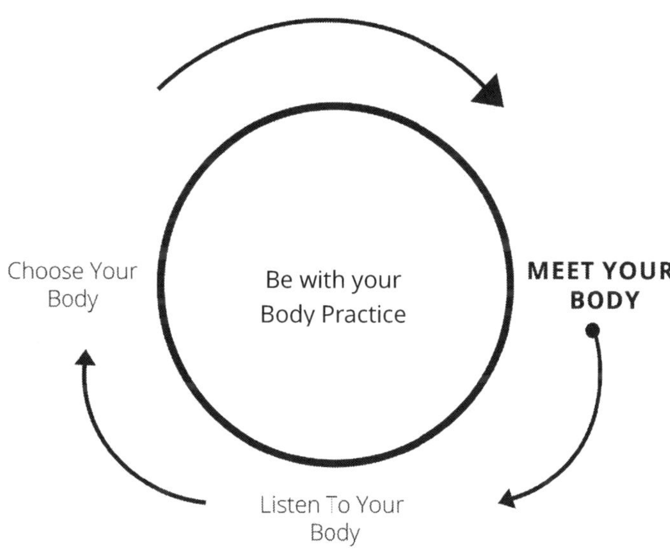

Meet your body—Place your attention and notice your body

When you meet your body, you place your attention directly on it. Think of it like meeting someone for the first time. You take your attention away from whatever you are doing and direct it towards the person you are meeting. You have lots of options where to place your attention. For the *Be with your Body Practice*, you'll place that attention on your body. The outcome of meeting your body is you'll end up noticing. You'll notice different areas of your body. You'll notice what you see, hear or feel in your body.

Listen to your body— Physically sense your body

Listening to your body is the act of receiving the physical messages your body is sending you. When you listen to your body you are sensing your body. So often we say we *feel* cold when actually we are not emotionally feeling coldness. We are physically *sensing* coldness. We listen to our body in order to gain information it is sharing with us. Our body communicates with us by sending us sensations all day long.

Choose your body— Create your next moment

To choose is to recognize your options and pick one. The act of choosing is what you do until you choose again, ideally with mindfulness. When you choose to invest your time and energy with those you love in your life, those relationships grow deeper and more meaningful. And so it is with your relationship with your body. After you meet and listen to *your* body, you then get to choose what to do next, for your body.

In the chapters ahead, I'll be shedding light on how each of these steps contribute to your health and wellbeing. Working with each step by itself is a worthwhile and vibrant practice, rewarding you with new insights and revelations. When you begin to practice the three together—meet, listen and choose—you'll embark on creating a more powerful way to live life.

Please note that although the steps Meet, Listen and Choose are introduced in this particular order, they are actually interchangeable. You can start with any of the three steps and travel either clockwise or counterclockwise. I think of each step like an onramp of a traffic circle. You may find yourself entering into the process from any step, and travel through in any direction. Let's look at a few examples.

Scenario One

You love to play tennis, but the past few days your knee has been "acting up." A friend calls and asks if you want to play today. Using your *Be with your Body Practice*, you:

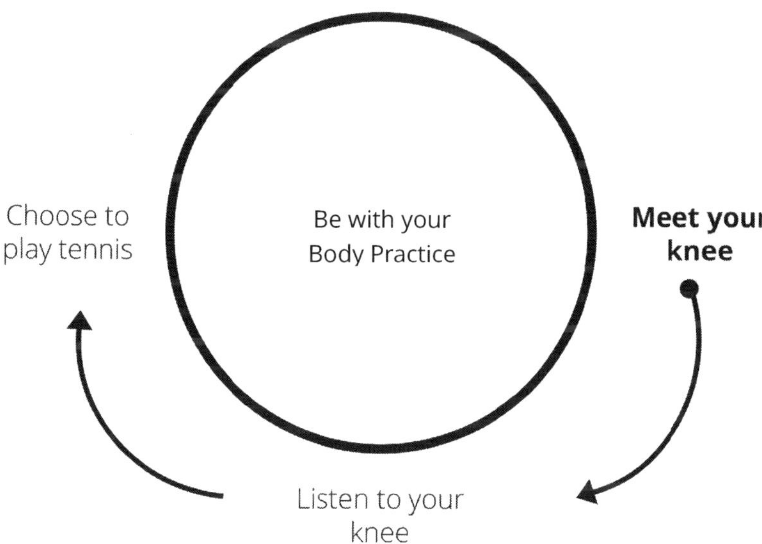

(Meet) You place your attention on your knee.

(Listen) You listen to how your knee is "physically feeling." You sense it.

(Choose) You choose to play tennis or not. You create your next moment.

Scenario Two

Your friend calls and asks you to play tennis.

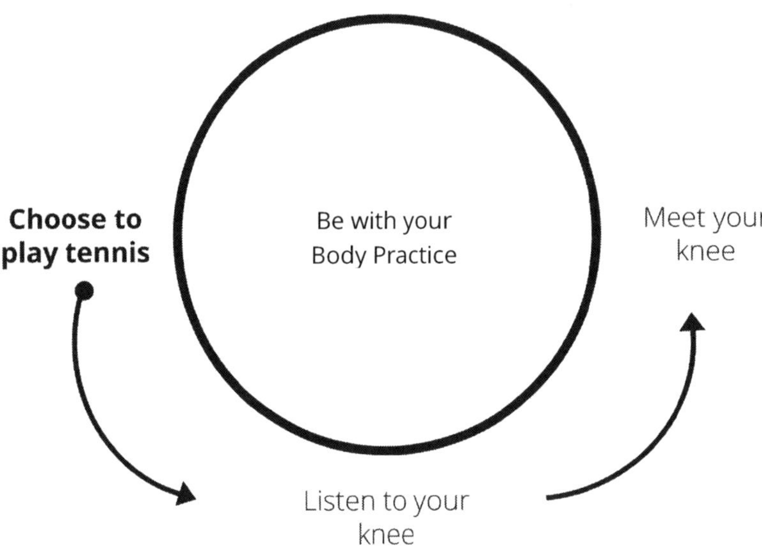

(Choose) You say, "I'd love to."

(Listen) While playing tennis you listen to your knee feeling a little sore.

(Meet) You notice your knee hurts when you lunge forward for the ball.

Scenario Three

You think to yourself, "I'd love to play tennis today, but let me see how my knee feels."

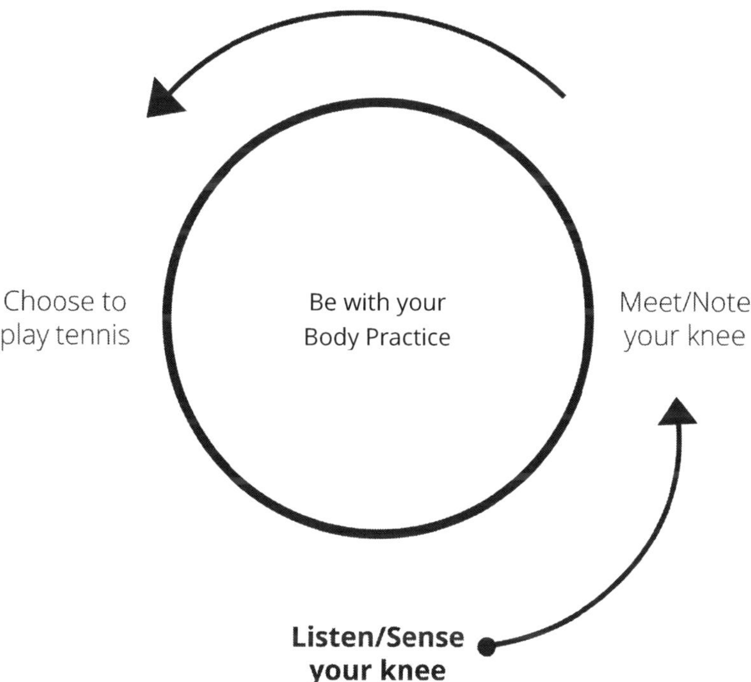

(Listen) You sense your knee while doing some knee bends.

(Meet) You place your attention on your knee and notice it feels great!

(Choose) You choose to play tennis.

All of these scenarios are perfect ways to be with your body!

The *Be with your Body Practice* not only has various directions, but is also continual. As you get comfortable with the process, you'll use it repeatedly. You'll continue to Meet, Listen and Choose—in any order.

For example, using the scenario from above, you can continually use the process to sense how your knee is feeling while you are playing tennis. You can discover if a certain movement irritates your knee by placing your attention on your knee and listening to it. And then you can choose how to help it feel better—anything from stopping early, playing less aggressively, to icing it when you get home or booking a massage—there are so many choices when you keep checking with your body!

As you read the individual chapters, I encourage you to spend some time with each step and play with that particular practice. Heed the word practice. All three steps get easier with practice. You'll find you can meet your body the more often you do so. Listening to your body may seem relatively new, but trust you have been doing it all your life (like each time you run to the bathroom, or feel a hunger pang). As far as choosing goes, research shows we make up to 35,000 choices a day! The difference here is I'm asking you to consider choosing for your body. What would make your body feel better? The powerful part of the *Be with your Body Practice* is you are now doing each and all of these steps with consciousness while including your body.

CHAPTER 07

Meet Your Body

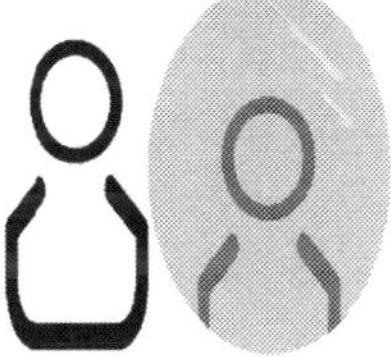

In previous chapters, by noticing your thoughts, beliefs and stories, you've been able to "meet yourself." You've been placing your attention on how you think, what you feel, and ultimately how you talk to yourself about your body. You could say you've spent the last few chapters meeting your mind and emotions. Now it is time to meet your body!

Meet your Body is one step in the *Be with your Body Practice.* It asks you to take your attention and place it on your body. This step is similar to meeting a person for the first time. When we meet another we look towards them, place our attention on them, and greet them. Typically we smile, maybe extend a hand, and say "hello."

When meeting your body, you are taking the same approach. You are directing your attention away from other distractions and placing it on your body, body area, or body part to say "hello."

Placing our attention, whether on someone else or our body, is like using a spotlight. When we place our attention on them, they arc illuminated. Being in the light enables us to notice them, to gather information based on what we see, hear, smell and feel.

How Do You Begin?

Start by clearing your mind, even if for a few fleeting moments. Clearing your mind is a practice in and of itself! Use any imagery that helps you detach from your thoughts. Next, take your spotlight of attention and place it on your body. Imagine shining the spotlight right on a certain body part. Try it now. Place your attention and notice your hands. Now move the spotlight and draw your attention to your left foot. Can you narrow your spotlight to notice the heel of your left foot? Now draw the spotlight back and notice your entire lower body. Relatively simple, right? In fact, you may be thinking, is that it? Yes, it is. Simply direct your mind to your body and notice. I encourage you to practice sustaining your attention longer to notice more details. For example, if you are noticing your right hand, you may develop the ability to notice the veins on your hand, or the creases in your skin. You can notice the color variation or the shape your hand is making. The longer you are able to sustain placing your attention on your hand, the more information you will begin to gather.

Now, for a change of experience, take your attention away from your body and place it on the book. Not your hands touching the book, but instead notice the actual book (or tablet). What do you notice? The shape of the letters on the page? The color of the paper? The screen brightness? Or the garbage truck that just pulled up and is making a racket!

Can you get a sense of how you can meet whatever you choose? You can take in a broader picture, like placing your attention on your entire body, or focus on a smaller area like your hands (or nails), all the while gathering information.

Notice Common Tendencies

There are a few common tendencies that happen when a person meets their body, whether it be for the first time or the thousandth. One tendency is for your mind to chat up a lengthy commentary or draw conclusions. For example, you may place your attention on your feet when you walk upstairs, only to hear your mind chatter on about how much you "don't like your feet," and "boy, you have feet like your father," and "huh, I wonder if I'll have foot surgery like Dad..." and on and on. If this happens, and it undoubtedly will, simply give your creative mind a wink and redirect your attention back to your body. By using the spotlight imagery, you can imagine your commentary and conclusions as thoughts outside your spotlight's beam of light. The commentary may be in the room with you, but in the dark background.

Another potential challenge is your ability to sustain your attention on what you are meeting. It is so easy to place your attention somewhere, then within a few moments jump to a new spot and place your attention somewhere else. Or get distracted. You may hear a noise, wonder about email, or follow your mind on some wayward tangent. It is like a spotlight at a circus. One minute the spotlight is on the clown and the next minute the high-wire act. And you know what? For our brain this is pretty normal because our brain is wired to be ready for action and has the ability to shift focus quickly. We also get lots of practice moving our attention around quickly, especially in our world of instant messaging and "multi-tasking" (which is really our amazing brain switching focus faster than we can notice).
condition, thus helping her body heal faster. She could struggle and suffer less—and so could her body.

There are many benefits of meeting your body. In the moment, simply placing your attention on one thing is physically relaxing to your nervous system; a mini-meditation of sorts. Also, as you practice placing your attention specifically on your body, you'll gather loads of juicy information to help you make choices about what is good for you and what is not. As you practice, you'll come to understand how in order to be with your body you must, at some point, meet your body.

Ask Yourself and Journal...

When I ask you to meet your body, what pops into your mind? Does it feel silly? Exciting? Confusing?

Close your eyes and place your attention on your body. I invite you to introduce yourself to your body, similar to how you would when meeting another for the first time. Write down what you say to your body.

Home Practice: Use the Energy Handshake

What's the proper way to meet somebody? With a handshake, of course! And that is what we are going to do with your body; we are going to use the energy of your attention to practice saying hello to your body. I invite you to read these words and then close your eyes and energetically introduce yourself to your body. Practice sustaining your attention on your body (or body part), just like when you meet a new person.

Close your eyes and take a few fuller-than-normal breaths. Let yourself grow quiet in your mind and also your body. In order to create an energy handshake, you're going to place you attention, like a spotlight, as you introduce yourself to your body. Take your spotlight and introduce yourself to your feet. Notice and meet your feet. Next travel up through your lower legs, knees and thighs and say hello. Energetically, use your mind to reach your body. Taking your own time, travel up through your pelvis, your spine, stomach area, chest area and upper back. Say hello. Linger as long as you like, giving these parts of your body your attention. From there, travel up through your neck, throat, jaw and face. Feel free to be as detailed as you wish, saying hello to your nose, eyes, and ears. Next, let your spotlight of attention travel down one or both of your arms, inviting you to say hello to your shoulder blades, shoulders, upper arms, elbows, and down to your hands. The order doesn't matter, simply allow yourself time to place your attention on each part of your body and say hello. Finish up by creating a spotlight big enough to encapsulate your entire body. Use this spotlight to say hello to all of your organs, blood, bones, ligaments, skin, and all the squishy tissues residing beneath your skin. End with a "Hello, Body" or any other phrase that comes to you.

Ask Yourself and Journal...

Write how it felt to meet your body with an energy handshake...

CHAPTER 08

Listen To Your Body

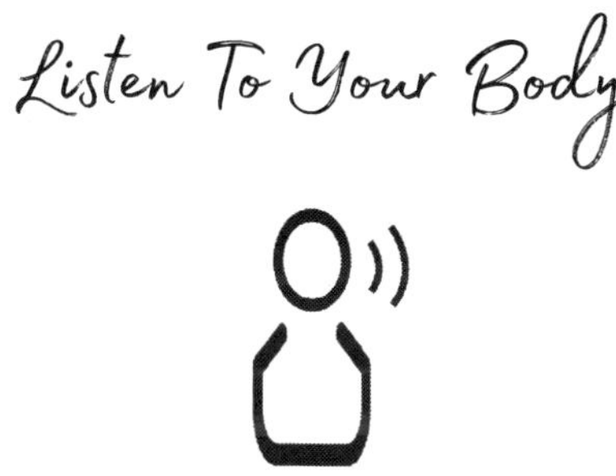

When I was growing up in rural Idaho, we had a party line. Yes, back in the day when the phone hung on the wall with a long cord, which I'd stretch as far as possible for some privacy. A party line, if you can believe it, was an actual telephone land line shared between neighbors, something common for homes in rural communities "way back when." I'd pick up the phone to call my best friend Kim, only to hear another conversation on the line. I'd check back a few minutes later, hear my neighbors still talking, and hang up the phone again. This usually went on much longer than my impatient, teenage self could tolerate. I wanted those others to get off the line, so I could have a conversation with my friend!

Well, something like this also plays out in our bodies. Because our mind or emotions are constantly on the line feeding us information, our bodies can hardly get our attention, let alone get a conversation started.

In today's world the struggle for our bodies to communicate with us is like an unmuted conference call, where inevitably at some point people talk at the same time, words overlapping, making it impossible to understand the conversation. When this happens we hear different voices but can't clearly hear the message.

To get happy with your body, you'll need to be with your body. And a big part of being with your body is learning to listen to your body so you can understand its messages.

Have you stopped listening to your body? Or perhaps you're really not sure what listening to your body means? Well, whether you dialed into an old-fashioned party line or today's conference call, it's time to make a direct connection with your body.

How Do You Begin?

Now that you've had a chance to meet and greet your body, the next natural step to being with your body is to listen. What better way to begin building a relationship with your body than to listen to what it has to reveal. But how exactly do you do that? Well, it's really no different than how you listen to your friends, family, colleagues and peers: you place your attention on them. And you avoid being distracted, so you can receive what the other has to share with you.

Doesn't that seem easy? But how often have you asked, "Can you repeat that, I wasn't listening," or thought to yourself, "What was their name again?" Even though we hear others frequently throughout the day, many times we are not fully receiving what we hear. In one of my workshops recently, an attendee pointed out that the exact letters are in both the words Listen and Silent. And yes, a big part of being a great listener is our ability to create a silence within us so we can receive the other's message.

And so it is with listening to your body. In order to listen to your body you place your attention on your body, remove distractions, and become receptive to the messages your body is sharing with you.

So, if it's that easy, what gets in the way?

Our lack of silence.

All too often we have "party-line" noise that comes when we think, feel, judge, question, and create responses—when we are being asked to simply, listen. Our minds are so busy, busy,

busy that creating the space to be receptive and listen to our body can be a straight-up struggle. Any of these scenarios sound familiar?

Oh, it's 3pm and I haven't eaten all day.

Hmm, I have no idea how I got that big bruise.

Yes, now that you ask, I've been feeling really low energy the past few weeks.

How Your Body Communicates

Listening to your body is a challenge because your body speaks in its own unique language. Your body communicates with you by sending physical sensations. These sensations reveal to you what your body is experiencing, right now. Sensations share your body's needs, desires and current experience. They are your body's physical messages to you.

I'm thirsty, I need water.

I'd love to move, take me for a walk.

I have a flu virus, I need to rest.

You were born with the ability to listen and respond to your body. You were born with the ability to sense physical sensation. As a baby, you cried when you sensed hunger, or when the skin on your bottom was uncomfortable due to a soiled or wet diaper. As a toddler, maybe you fussed over itchy tags at the collar of your shirt. As a school-age child you could explore the texture of sand, dirt, mud, or clay in your hands or the sensation of warm, bubbly bath water against your skin. As you grew up you continually explored and further developed what was pre-programmed from birth, your ability to sense your body.

Sensing your body is the act of listening to your body's physical messages (sensations).

With exquisite harmony, your body "talks" to you by relaying its real-time, physical experiences. You may say, "I feel cold," when actually you are "sensing coldness." In this case, you are listening with the largest organ of your body, your skin, and receiving this message on a physical level---not because you thought about it or imagined it, but because you actually listened to what your body shared with you.

Think of yourself in a shoe store trying on different pairs of shoes. By sampling multiple pairs of shoes, you can tell which pair, brand and size feels good and which one doesn't. You notice the amount of cushion the insole has, the texture of the fabric. You sense the pressure against the structure of your feet. Some people can even tell if a shoe is heavier in weight than they prefer. All in all, by trying on a variety of shoes, you can tell if a shoe feels too tight, too loose, or just not right. Is only your mind determining all this information? Nope, it is your body, specifically your foot, sharing its experience with you while you, in your momentary silence, listen to the message.

Converse with Your Body

All this listening and sharing begins to look and sound an awful lot like conversation. Whether we are listening and sharing with a friend or our body, we are engaging in communication. And communication typically helps us gather more information, which leads to better understanding. No different than having a conversation with your friend, you can have a conversation with your body.

You send out a request: *I want to know how these shoes feel on my feet.*

Your message goes out to your feet and asks: *Feet, how do you feel?*

You wait and listen for messages from your feet.

Your toes tell you they have enough room to wiggle comfortably. Your arch tells you it feels well-supported. Your skin tells you there is the just-right amount of pressure and no places where the skin feels pinched.

As you listen to these messages (sensations) from your feet, you've gathered enough information to accept these shoes feel good. And then you are free to make a choice to purchase them or not. You asked about the shoes and your body reported back to you via sensations, its present-moment experience.

In this example, you led the conversation. *You* were curious about how the shoes felt on your feet. *You* were asking your body for feedback. *You* were taking the time to quiet your mind and emotions to listen to your body. *You* asked, while the body revealed, and *you* listened to what your body had to say.

Can your body lead the conversation? Can your body reveal itself in ways that get your attention? It sure can and does! For example, how did you know you needed new running shoes? Did your feet begin to reveal they were sore? Did you notice, at some point, the soles of your feet telling you they were tender? Or maybe you noticed another body part, like your knees, starting to feel less than pleasurable. After a long day of standing and working, I remember my mom saying, "I have to sit down—my pups (feet) are really barking at me." Yes, your body can start the conversation with you by sending you many sensations. Your body sends you sensations and you end up "hearing" them.

- With a *body-driven* conversation, your *body* sends out sensations and you receive them, without having asked for them.

- With a *you-driven* conversation, *you* are asking your body for feedback by listening to your body and asking your body what it is experiencing.

Both methods are important ways you communicate with and thus build a relationship with your body. Whether you start the conversation or your body does, it is a two-way conversation between you and your body. Communication between you and your body is a lifesaving, life-enhancing, and valuable gift you use each and every day. Impressively, communication between you and your body happens with relative ease, somewhat automatically, unconsciously, and without much celebration or fanfare. Your body sends you physical messages all day long:

- I'm sleepy—Aha! A sensation!
- I'm hungry—Aha! Another one!
- This chair is too hard—Yup, a physical message!
- I need to pee—You get the picture, right?

Did your *body* tell you that you were sleepy? Did your stomach growl and send you hunger pangs? Did you receive a twinge in your lower back letting you know your seat was uncomfortable?

Or did *you* start the conversation and check in with your body?

- Do I need to pee before I get on this airplane?
- It's noon, am I hungry for lunch?
- Wow, it's getting late, am I sleepy?

Many of your daily choices are based on this two-way communication system between you and your body. You make decisions all the time based on the messages you are receiving.

Even as I sit here writing, I've noticed several of my body's physical messages.

- I was thirsty, so I reached for my water bottle and took a drink of water.
- My thumb ached from holding the pencil and writing, so I shook out my hand and loosened my grip.
- I felt stiffness in my spine from sitting, so I did a few spinal twists.

All these tiny, minute adjustments and actions, seemingly inconsequential, happen without much thought because I practice listening to my body and responding to its desires and needs. What once started as a practice has now become a habit for me and I am accustomed to placing my attention on my body and listening for its physical messages. I then make a choice to do something to help my body feel better.

All relationships have a level of communication, even unhealthy relationships. Great relationships have clear, understandable and honest communication. We feel heard. They feel heard. Both parties feel valued and choose to be with one another.

Cultivating a "Relationship Mindset," where you consciously develop a healthy relationship with your body based on communication, is the secret sauce to getting happy with your body.

We want to be happy with our bodies. Yet too often our approach is anything but relational. Instead we act punitively towards our body, punishing what our body is or isn't. Or we demand our body act and look a certain way without considering our body's perspective. As a society, we've done just about everything to change or improve how our bodies look, feel or perform, and we forget our body has a voice all its own. Listening to your body's physical messages is the way you discover what your body is experiencing. And whether the experience is healthy for it or not.

As you listen to your body, you can begin to relate to it, over and over again. The more often you listen and relate to your body, the healthier your relationship will become.

Awaken your Sensory Taste Buds

Circle which sensations you recognize as having experienced in your body. Also notice which ones seem foreign to you, as if your body has not likely experienced them (lately or never).

Airy
Achy
Bloated
Blocked
Breathless
Brittle
Bruised
Bubbly
Burning
Buzzy
Calm
Clammy
Clenched
Closed
Cold
Congested
Constricted
Contracted
Cool
Damp
Dense
Disconnected
Dizzy
Draining
Dry
Dull
Electric
Empty
Energized
Expansive
Faint
Floating
Flowing
Fluid
Flushed
Fluttery
Frozen
Full
Heavy
Hollow
Hot
Icy
Itchy
Jagged
Jittery
Knotted
Light
Mobile
Moist
Nauseous
Nervy
Numb
Open
Paralyzed
Pins & Needles
Pounding
Pressure
Prickly
Puffy
Pulsing
Queasy
Radiating
Raw
Referring
Relaxed
Releasing
Sensitive
Shaky
Shivery
Smooth
Sore
Spacey
Spacious
Stable
Still
Strong
Suffocating
Sweaty
Tender
Tense
Thick
Throbbing
Tight
Tingly
Trembling
Twitchy
Warm
Weak
Wobbly
Wooden

Keep this list close by. As you begin to listen to your body more closely, you can ask yourself which specific sensations your body is sending you. Is there a burning feeling down the back of your leg? Or is it tingly?

You can also use this list as a guide to create new sensations in your body. Grab a word, focus on a body part (or whole body) and begin to move with the sensation in mind. For example, become *fluid*. This can be a fun way to explore the different types of sensations you can physically feel in your body. What does it physically feel like when you move with a *spacious* ribcage? How about moving with the sensation of *heavy* legs. How about typing with tense shoulders? These all provide different physical experiences.

Notice Physical Sensations

There are countless ways to listen to your body. And though it may seem like a new skill, it isn't. You already know how. Most likely you are just a little out of practice. Perhaps you've forgotten how good it feels to be in and move your body. For some people, sensing their body while they move feels playful and freeing, like child play. For others, moving while sensing their body feels deeply reverent and meditative. I encourage you to be open to your own experience and recognize how your experience itself can change from day to day.

One way to listen to your body is to simply practice noticing the physical messages that occur throughout the day. Little things like your stomach growling when it is hungry, the sensation of having to use the bathroom, or walking to your car. Staying connected to and listening to the physical messages your body is sending you throughout the day helps you to be more responsive to your body, and therefore helps you to feel better.

Home Practice: Fine-Tune Your Listening Skills

Listed below are some simple and quick home practices designed to fine-tune your listening skills by specifically creating a variety of sensations. These six movement practices are "flavors" you can create when you move your body and listen to its physical messages. Getting to know these different flavors will enable you to become more sensitive to the messages your body is sending you. The more frequently you practice placing your attention on your body and asking it what it is physically feeling, the greater your capacity to listen to your body. Becoming a better listener will ultimately get you involved and on track to developing a deeper understanding of, and relationship with, your body. Below is just a sampling; you may discover more! You'll see in italics my experiences and notes I had when doing these exercises at home.

Sense Pressure

Give yourself a big hug. Squeeze your body and receive the physical feeling of pressure. Vary your pressure, applying a lot of pressure (squeezing hard) or a light amount. Lastly, like adjusting a volume dial, start with a light amount of pressure and sense what it feels like to create more pressure until you reach your max. Slowly, decrease pressure and notice the physical feeling in your body.

What does pressure physically feel like in your body? What did you sense? For example, *I sensed a squeezing against the skin of my upper back. I sensed my chest muscles contracting to squeeze me. I sensed my hands gripping.* Do your best to use the words "sense and notice."

Sense Shape

Stand up and make the largest shape you can with your body. Expand yourself fully and receive what it physically feels like to be a large shape. Hold the shape for a few moments until the shape you've made and its size registers with you. Next, make the smallest shape you can get yourself into. You don't have to squeeze yourself here (that would be adding pressure). Instead, just let your body fold and shrink. Be physically small. Sense what being a small shape feels like in your body. Lastly, explore the sensation of growing from your small shape to your largest shape, receiving the sensations of changing your shape.

What does creating different shapes with your body physically feel like? What did you sense as a big shape? What did you sense as a small shape? *For example, as a large shape I sensed my bones feeling very long and pointed. I sensed space in my body. As a small shape, I sensed my breath pushing my ribcage against my thighs.*

Sense Texture

For this exercise, you are going to sense moving with texture within your body rather than touching a specific texture. I invite you to move a body part smoothly; could be your spine or maybe your arms and hands. Imagine the texture of something flowing or silky. Receive what your body physically feels like moving smoothly. Next, create the opposite sensation; move a body part with jaggedness or sharpness. Continue playing with moving your body from smoothness to jaggedness and receive the different sensations in your body.

What did you physically feel in your body when you moved smoothly? For example, *I sensed a pulling sensation across my chest and down my arms. I sensed clumsiness in my shoulder blades (yes, even though I was moving smoothly!). Just because I was moving smoothly doesn't mean all my sensations were smooth. This is a good practice for being present with your body without judgment. Allow yourself to physically feel sensations in your body. For me, I sensed a jarring, pulling across the inside of my elbows. And the longer I moved this way, I noticed my breath became jagged too.*

Sense Weight

Now it is time to explore sensing body weight. Find a body part or area and invite it to feel physically heavy. Now receive what heaviness physically feels like. Then, while moving your body, change the weight of that body part to feel light. Receive the physical feeling of being light. Feel free to practice changing from light to heavy and how your body physically feels different.

What did you sense in your physical body when you experienced heaviness? For example, *I used my head. When moving my heavy head, I sensed a slow pulling sensation along my back muscles. I sensed heavy arms, too. When I changed to moving my head with lightness, I had the sensation of floating.*

A quick check-in: For some of these exercises you may find you want to describe the mental or emotional ways you feel. For example, with heaviness you may want to say, *I feel depressed*. Or with the lightness, *I feel inspired*. These are emotions. Do your best to place your attention on your physical structure and describe the physical experience your body is having.

Sense Speed

Your body can move at a variety of speeds, and each speed provides you with unique sensations. Whether with a body part or your entire body, move at a certain speed. Receive what your body physically feels when moving at that speed. Then change the speed and sense other sensations.

What do you sense, and where are you sensing it, when you move slowly? And then quickly? *For me, as I squatted slowly I sensed my thigh muscles engage and squeeze. When I squatted up and down faster, I sensed my knees opening and closing.*

Sense Distance

Thankfully, your body can also navigate distance. There are times when you need to reach to grab a book on a shelf, and times when you are barely squeezing through a tight space between two chairs. For this experience, walk with very long strides, increasing the distance between all your limbs, especially your feet. Sense what your body is physically experiencing when you create distance. Next, switch to the opposite, taking very small steps and narrowing the distance between your feet. Receive the difference between both sensations.

What do you sense in your body when you create distance? *For me, I sensed pushing off my feet more and a swinging sensation in my arms. When I changed to a very small stride, I sensed a rubbing between my inner thighs and a tightness across the top of my ankle.*

CHAPTER 09

Once you meet your body and begin to listen to it, your next step in the *Be with your Body Practice* is to Choose. Do I keep shoveling snow even though my shoulder hurts, or not? Do I run an extra mile, or walk? Am I hungry for chocolate cake, or even hungry at all? Meeting your body, listening to your body and choosing your body creates the full circle of developing an ongoing relationship with your body—where you are continually relating to your body.

Imagine a friend who is interested in spending more time together. She asks you to lunch but your work has been really crazy so you have to say no. A few weeks later, she invites you out for happy hour, something you've enjoyed together in the past. Again, you have plans and have to say you are unavailable. By the third time your friend reaches out to you, you can tell she is upset and the relationship is starting to suffer. It's not like you've meant to hurt her feelings, but your choices have steered you away from what's important in having a meaningful friendship: being with one another.

Now consider that you can listen to your body, but if you continually make decisions that separate you from your body, the relationship with it will suffer too. This often looks like illness or injury. Or gaining unwanted weight. Or feeling out of shape. Your body has been sending you messages, wanting to connect. Maybe you've heard them, those little hints (sensations) that your body isn't feeling great, and even so, you've made a choice to choose something else. Just like our friendships in life, our relationship with our body is nurtured by what choices we make.

What About Choice?

You have it. I have it. Most of us have the luxury of choice, certainly around some things. That doesn't mean we always *feel* like we have a choice, or feel like making a choice. Not all choices are easy to make. Among the choices you have, in the course of your day, how often do you choose your body? Hmm, not much? After all, we have responsibilities. We have obligations. We have the day-to-day grind of showing up, digging in and getting done what needs to be done. Our lists are long and our time is short. Choice sounds like a luxury. Who's got time to consider a choice? And quite frankly, choice can scare the you-know-what out of us. What if I make the wrong one? It seems easier to simply forget we have choices, a case of choice-amnesia.

How often do you place your attention on your choices? When was the last time you entertained a choice? Did you wine and dine it? Look at it under different lighting? Shake hands and introduce yourself to your available choices? Or do you blast right past Choice and beeline straight to Decision?

Choice is different than its swifter relative, Decision. Choice has swagger. Choice mingles. Choice loves attention and wants to be noticed. Choice is provocative, and ever the instigator. "Look at me, I'm a choice. Do you desire me?" And each choice has its own appeal and individuality. Each choice welcomes you to its unfolding potential, whether the journey be relatively insignificant or life-changing.

Have you left choice in the dust? Have you sped right by with barely a glance? Maybe a little head nod, "Yes, I see you, Choice, but I'm in a hurry. I need to get to a Decision." Besides, many of us are familiar with decisions. We've come to the same decisions over and over again. Or we've taken a fraction of a second to glance at choice only to get back in the driver's seat with the GPS headed straight to the same familiar decision.

It's all very understandable. Making decisions has a certain appeal. Deciding can give us a feeling of confidence. We feel safe and assured making decisions, especially familiar ones. Funny thing though, so often we make the same decisions, while wanting a different result. We want a change, yet with a serious case of choice-amnesia, we end up acting the same way. Then when nothing changes, we feel angry. Or disappointed. Not surprisingly, when we head straight to the same decision, we usually get the same outcome.

Do you have choice-amnesia? Have you simply forgotten you can entertain multiple choices? You can meander amidst an entire population of choices.

Choosing is different than deciding.

I choose you is different than *I decide* on you.

Try it. Stand up with your legs shoulder-width apart, like the super-hero that you are. Now, extend your arm fully at chest-height, point your index finger like a laser pointer, and say, "I choose you." Feel the exactness, the power of the stance, your open chest, and your elegantly simple statement of I choose you.

Now try it again but this time say, *I decide on you.*

What do you notice? Does deciding feel a little heavy? To me it feels a little weighty, with a dash of burden. Totally un-fun. Whereas choosing embodies all of me: my heart, my spirit, my mind and my body. I decide with my head, but I choose with all of me.

What is Choosing Your Body?

Take a few deep breaths, 'cuz I have a big statement: If you want to get happy with your body, you need to start choosing your body.

Sounds simple enough. However, I have found following through on this is a real bugger. Yet there really is no way around it. It's pretty tough to feel healthy in your body if your choices are not healthy. It's difficult to feel satisfied with your body if you choose to focus on every little thing you don't like. You cannot find peace with your body if you continually fight it. Too often we say we want to get happy with our body, but we choose work, our kids, our partners, the laundry, on and on. We keep saying, "I want to get happy with my body," while continuing to choose something different. In our minds we still want it, then get disappointed and frustrated when we aren't getting what we want. Have we really chosen our body? Have we really chosen the outcome we want?

I wish choosing your body was a one-time, single-serving, check-it-off-your-to-do-list task. The beauty of choosing your body is you get the opportunity to choose it over and over again. You get a chance to choose your body a little each day, because your body is a living, breathing, evolving system that is never quite the same. Like a plant, you can't just water it once and expect a beautiful bloom.

Choosing your body may not be what you think. In fact, let's unpack this loaded question right here. What would it look like if you were choosing your body? Does choosing your body mean you're eating all the right food? Getting eight hours of perfect sleep? Does it look like a long checklist of "well, if I'm going to be healthy, I've got *to do all this*"? Quite the contrary! You don't have to spend the rest of your life choosing the healthiest food on the buffet line, taking a fistful of vitamins or doing countless yoga or Pilates classes. You don't need to be a size smaller, fit into your wedding dress from a decade ago, or run a half-marathon. Choosing your body isn't a to-do list you (or anyone else) creates for you.

Here's the thing:

Choosing your body is not just about what you do. Choosing your body is also about being with your body and *choosing from that place*.

Hmm, excuse me, what place are you talking about?

That place. A Be with your Body place. That place you've been practicing. That place where you meet your body with your attention, and listen to your body in order to navigate your choices.

One helpful way to become more body-centered is to notice when you are choosing from your head (mind). This sounds like, "I *think* I will choose..." or "I *always* choose…" Then there are your emotions, influencing your choices away from being body-centered. For example, when you choose out of duty, or a sense of responsibility, or that very common emotion, guilt. "I *should* choose..."

Certainly when it comes to our health, eating right, and exercise, there is considerable pressure to constantly make the right choice. So often I hear people say, "I know what to do, if only I would make the right choice."

Sound familiar? I should not have this second (or third) glass of wine. I should lose ten (or fifty) pounds and get off cholesterol medicine. I should…stop smoking, eat more vegetables, do high intensity training, take my vitamins, drink more water, eat more fiber, have sex three times a week, recycle, donate, volunteer, read books and understand current news events...and on and on.

Ask Yourself and Journal...

What are your top "body should dos" that weigh on you the most? I find that most of us have a handful that haunt us. What are yours? You can write as many as you like, though I'm asking for the ones that take up too much space in your psyche and lead to some bumps and bruises because you beat yourself up over them.

My top body-oriented should dos when "should-ing" on myself are:

1)

2)

3)

4)

5)

Choose To Be Kind to Yourself

What you place your attention on grows stronger in your life. Using your noticing skills, you have a valuable opportunity to recognize the way you talk to yourself, especially around your choices.

A mentor of mine had a telling philosophy: "You cannot get out of pain by inflicting more pain."

Let that sink in. You are in pain. You want out of pain, so you do things that bring you more pain with the hope you'll get out of pain. If you keep feeling and choosing pain, my friend, you are going to get what you inflicted—pain. This also goes for emotional pain, where we repeatedly hurt our own feelings based on how we talk to ourselves.

If you've set yourself up to only have one glass of wine, but choose to have two and then inflict more pain on yourself by berating yourself and feeling guilty, more than likely you'll feel so bad you'll need another glass of wine! Inflicting more pain on yourself will not help you make a better choice the next time.

Align Your Choices

What can you do if you are not making the choices you want? Give some time and attention to these options:

Notice your choice—Avoid leaving the choice hiding in the dark. Be kind to yourself and shine the light on it. Gently inquire. Why do I want this? What am I expecting of myself? What am I hoping to fix by making this choice?

Notice your options—Oftentimes we give ourselves rules to make choosing easier. For example, you might say you want to have only one glass of wine. Instead of focusing on the "rule," consider focusing on your options that will support what you desire. You could drink more slowly; fill your glass up halfway each time; use a beautiful, but smaller glass; turn it into a wine spritzer.

Check with your body—Continuing with the wine example, keep checking in with your body while you have your one glass of wine. Enjoy your one glass consciously; savor it.

Notice your mind, emotions and your body—What is going through your mind when you make this choice? How are you feeling about this choice? What are you sensing physically, before or after you make this choice?

Choose Your Next

Very few choices are final. Recognizing you have a multitude of options, and you have the power to choose any one of those options, can feel daunting. Keep in mind you get to choose again and again. You are able to choose and then pay attention to how that new choice plays out. You are continuously what I call "choosing your next"—your next step, your next moment. So even if your first choice doesn't reap what you desire, simply choose again.

From one of my favorite books, *Unraveling: Letting Go-Getting Well*, author Philip Greenfield writes "If you always do what you always did; you'll always get what you always got." Then there's the common phrase defining insanity as doing the same thing over and over and expecting different results. And of course, there is TV host and hard-ass, Dr Phil, who often asks his on-air guests, "How's that working for you?"

If you want to step in a new direction, you ultimately have to do that: make a different choice.

And likewise, if you are looking for a more *favorable* relationship with your body, then you must choose in *favor* of your body. If you want a more loving relationship with your body, then you must choose to act more lovingly towards your body. If you want a more peaceful relationship with your body, then you must choose what feels peaceful. Not perfectly, not each and every time. Simply more often than you currently do.

Consider a Variety of Choices

One of the most important considerations of choice is noticing there are a variety of them. There is conscious choice, where you are placing your full attention on your choice. Another is unconscious choice, where you are not paying attention to the choice you made. In addition to conscious and unconscious choice there are what I consider subsets of choices:

instincts, habits and reactions. For example, you may make a conscious choice to floss your teeth after every meal. Or you may react to a popcorn kernel getting between two molars and choose to floss your teeth. Or you may have a *habit* of flossing your teeth and barely notice you do it.

And though it is tempting to label these types of choices as either good or bad, or tell you which ones you should always make, I'm not going to do that. After all, many of us currently have habits that work for us! And we have reactions that work in our favor. Or we do something instinctually and it leads to something surprisingly wonderful. Life is so full of choices that we make every single minute of the day, we certainly want some variety.

Many times what we choose directly results in what we get. But it may not always be what *we need or yearn* to receive. For example, I might choose to comfort myself by eating cake when I feel sad, but afterward I feel regretful over my choice and sense my stomach feeling stuffed and nauseous. Ultimately, that choice does not lead to me feeling better, or emotionally soothed. I chose the cake for comfort, but that's not what I got.

Often when our outcome is something different than what we intended, we beat ourselves up for that choice. We talk nasty to ourselves, berating ourselves for making a stupid choice. When that happens, practice the *Be with your Body Practice* and meet your body by placing your attention on it. Then listen to the messages your body is sending you. Finally, make a choice for your next moment, the very next moment. Not, "next time I won't eat that cake." No, that's choosing too far in the future. I'm asking you to choose for the very next moment. Will you choose to continue berating yourself? Or will you choose to recognize what you really need? Will you choose kindness, because that is what you really need now? Will you choose comfort? Forgiveness? Most of us would never think to berate, bitch out or talk nasty to a friend when that friend is feeling sad, down or ashamed. Our natural tendency is to listen to, emotionally comfort, and lift our friends up. We remind them of all the good in themselves and in their lives. We encourage them to forgive themselves. We say things in hopes of easing their burden and their suffering.

If you make a choice you're unhappy with, treat yourself like your own best friend. Be kind. Be forgiving. There's always another chance to choose.

For example, I was visiting my sister in Arizona. We went out one late afternoon shopping, because frankly shopping with my sister is always fun. I needed a pair of shoes to match a new outfit. We got to the shoe department and I tried on several pairs of cute shoes. I'm incredibly particular about how my feet feel in shoes, and even though I fell in love with a cute pair of black flats, after walking in them I noticed they hurt my big toe on my right foot. Darn, do I buy them and just put up with the pain? Well, I'm pretty sensitive to my feet and I really value them being happy so I did not choose the shoes. Even though I personally was disappointed, I knew my feet would be better off.

I chose in favor of my body.

Next, we went to another store where I found another adorable pair of charcoal gray shoes. They fit great and felt comfortable, too!

Hurray! A win-win for both my body and me.

Eventually we headed to dinner. Sigh, the cheeseburger sounded really good to ME. But I had just gotten over the stomach flu about a week earlier and my stomach was still recovering. I, Jill, would have loved a burger, but when I checked in with my body about eating that burger, I noticed my stomach did a little flip-flop, sending me the message of "please, no burger tonight!"

Sigh…fish tacos instead.

I chose in favor of my body.

Actually, the fish tacos were delicious and my sister gave me a bite of her burger and that was just the right amount to satiate my burger desire.

Yes, another win-win for what I desired (bite of burger) and what was okay with my body! After dinner, I asked to go to a frozen yogurt shop. I wasn't hungry but I was craving a sweet, frozen treat.

I chose in favor of Jill. I personally wanted frozen yogurt even though my body had just eaten.

We got there and I was nearly giddy with all the wonderful flavors and variety of toppings—nearly all sweet (ugh, sugar, my personal downfall). Lately I've noticed my body prefers less milk products, so I did choose a lactose-free yogurt.

I chose for my body.

I headed over to the toppings and picked my favorite two and tossed them on. Even though the 8-year-old in me wanted to pile on heaps of M&M's, Oreo cookie crumbs and caramel sauce, I respect my body too much to overload it with *that* much sugar. So I took a small scoop of each—a happy medium between enjoying my dessert without going overboard.

The entire afternoon and evening I was engaged with checking in with my body, sensing how it felt and then choosing based on what I wanted and what my body needed. I didn't choose my body 100% of the time, and I didn't choose what I thought I "should" choose in order to be "healthy" (like salad for dinner and skipping the frozen yogurt.)

I share these examples of how I use the *Be with your Body Practice* in my daily life so you can begin to insert the practice into your own life. Meet your body by placing attention on it, listen to it the best you can, and then negotiate the array of choices based on what is best for your body and also what feels good to you, personally. Because not only do you want your body to be happy but you personally want to be happy, too. You'll notice choices are constantly fluctuating, negotiating, blending and adapting. You're not perfect. You don't have to choose the vision of eating or exercising perfectly. You can choose to acknowledge your desires while understanding, respecting and appreciating your body's desires and needs, too.

Travel Around the Practice

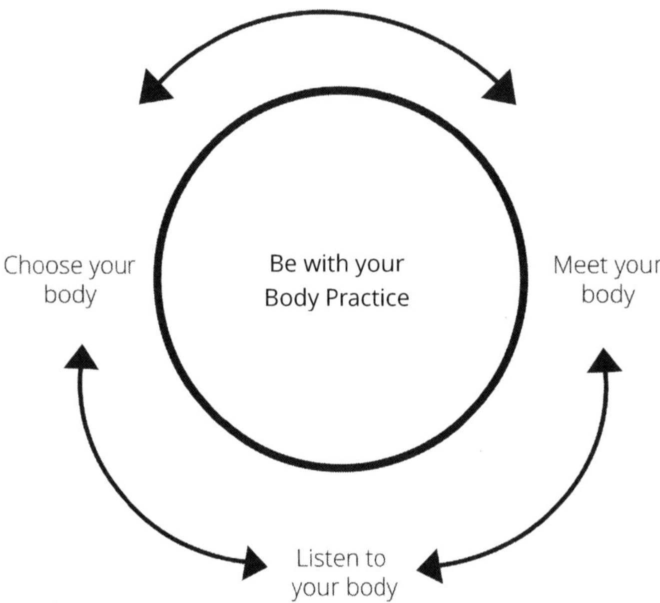

The *Be with your Body Practice* is circular because it is continual; a never-ending process where you Meet your body, Listen to your body and ultimately Choose your body! After you've made your choice, jump back into the circular process and meet your body again. Place your attention on your body and ask how this choice is working out for it. Listen as your body reveals to you how your choice influences and affects it. Is the outcome of your choice pleasurable? Safe? Valuable to you and your body? These are all positive outcomes.

What if you didn't get the outcome you wanted?

Go back and place your attention on your body, listen again and then choose your next. The circular nature of the process enables you to constantly adapt to what you learn. Bodies are always changing, sometimes noticeably but most of the time not, and bodies can be unpredictable. What was good for it last month may not feel good for it this month. I encourage you to be unattached to your outcomes. What if your choice didn't work out so great for your body? Do your best to begin anew by meeting your body, listening to it and making a different choice.

I hope the *Be with your Body Practice* helps you engage with all three of these life-changing practices and guides you toward making positive transformations that move you in the direction of your desires. Use the process not as end points to complete, but as constant markers for recalibration along your journey. You do not need to practice the *Be with your Body Practice* each and every moment of the day. Instead, infuse your practice into certain moments. Or insert it into an area of your life you'd like to better understand. Use the process as a tool to live with, not a rule to live by. Let the practice of Meet, Listen, and Choose be a guided practice of enlightening—or in-light-in-ing—allowing more light in so you can discover how to live in, learn from and love your body, once and for all!

Ask Yourself and Journal...

What do you notice about your choices involving your body? Are you making choices that align with your desired outcomes? What choices don't align?

Do you recognize within yourself a tendency to make the same choices, hoping this time it will work out for you? For example, joining another gym in hopes of exercising more consistently?

Take one thing in regards to your body that you'd like to transform. This could be a specific physical issue like lowering your cholesterol, or an emotional issue like feeling at peace around food. Now brainstorm a variety of ways you could approach enlightening (bringing in light and awareness) this issue. For example, if I'd like to eat less sugar I could force myself to not eat sugar, throw out everything with sugar from my pantry, or join an online program that offers sugar-free recipes. Or I could educate myself on the harmful effects on the body when eating too much sugar, work with a hypnotherapist to reduce cravings, see a naturopath, or journal around what my emotional state is each time I reach for sugar. By doing this, you can then appreciate the many options you have to make your first choice.

Brainstorm your possible choices here:

Congratulations! You've done your best, learned a few things and gained valuable insights. Even though getting happy with your body is a continually adaptive process and practice, I do have one final journal exercise. I invite you to write a letter to your body. Perhaps it is a love letter; a gratitude entry; an apology or a confessional. Perhaps an alchemical mix of all of those. Take a moment. Consider your body, your health and your physical abilities. Consider how you've treated your body in your past and your intentions for the future. Now share this with your body.

Letter to your Body *Date:*

Now turn the page and write a letter from your body to you.

Letter from your Body

Date:

Notes

Final Thoughts

Throughout this book you have been discovering more about yourself, what it means to have a relationship mindset, and the benefits of fostering a meaningful relationship with your body. I know you are on the path to continually discover, cultivate and create your happy relationship with your body. With a little time and practice, you'll soon build a bridge of peace between you and your body by lovingly including your body in your choices. And all this will begin to foster comfort and ease that comes with understanding yourself, your thoughts, your feelings, and your body. From my heart to yours, I cheer you on and I praise the attention you've given yourself in reading this book and doing the journal exercises.

May you have renewed vision to see your ever-present beauty, fresh listening with which to absorb your truth, and new sensations throughout your body to physically live in the gift of the present moment!

Wishing you Happiness,

Jill

FREE GIFT FROM JILL

WWW.JILLPAGANO.COM

Visit www.jillpagano.com to download your free copy of Jill's Happy Body Habit Starter Kit!

ABOUT THE AUTHOR

Jill Pagano is a speaker, author and consultant. For over 25 years she has been an ambassador for the human body, influencing countless individuals to improve their well-being through movement and mindfulness. She is creator of The Happy Body Habit®, an innovative corporate wellness program that transcends traditional diet and exercise. She has appeared on New Day Northwest television show and contributed to Seattle Women's Magazine and Pacific Northwest Magazine.

Jill is certified through The American College of Sports Medicine and holds a Bachelor of Science degree in Communication.

A mother of two, she lives in Washington State with her partner Joel, and a too-quick-for-her-liking emptying nest.

To discuss speaking and/or corporate wellness opportunities, please contact Jill.

Email:	**Website:**	**LinkedIn:**	**Facebook:**
Jill@JillPagano.com	JillPagano.com	www.linkedin.com/in/JillPagano/	Facebook.com/JillFPagano

35701682R10102

Made in the USA
Middletown, DE
09 February 2019